One More Life Chance

How to support
the journey from trauma
to transformation

Mark Escott

First published in Great Britain in 2019 by
Rethink Press (www.rethinkpress.com)

Cover image © Shutterstock | Stockish

Printed and bound by CPI Group (UK) Ltd, Croydon, CR0 4YY

DISCLAIMER: Rethink Press Limited is not
connected with the charity National Schizophrenia
Fellowship, known as Rethink Mental Illness.

Praise

Mark Escott has courageously given us an honest and heart-wrenching summary of his life and the way in which his experiences have driven him to develop a model of education that genuinely provides life chances where otherwise there may be none. *One More Life Chance* is a powerful reminder that our lives are shaped not only by the experiences we have but by the relationships within them.

> – **Suzie Franklin** – Senior Consultant, Trauma Informed Schools UK

What Mark has experienced has become a valuable tool for helping others. Everyone connected with education and mental health needs to be provided with a copy of this book.

> – **Dr Chris Boyle** – Associate Professor in Inclusive Education and Psychology, University of Exeter

Reading anger, understanding barriers that traumatised children face, and the dialogue for misunderstood children are many of the insights that this book offers to the reader. The author presents his life story as the case study for arguing why the way education works needs to change. Children have the right to be understood and Mark helps you understand why traumatised children present anger to adults trying to help them.

– **Alison Shorer** – Founder and
Director of Articulacy

Contents

Foreword

Sometimes in life you find yourself meeting someone in a situation and asking yourself, 'What on earth are they doing here?' Meeting Mark at a drama and music project for highly vulnerable people (many of whom had multiple physical and learning disabilities) was just one of those occasions. Through my work, we designed and delivered a range of activities that were intended to provide stimulation, interaction and experiences that would be outside the limiting range of daily activities normally available to them. I suspect that our role was often to give their carers a break as much as anything else. We were a pretty arty, hippy and idealistic bunch who wanted to make a difference and change the world. Just two of us were employed to work with groups of up to twelve people, each of whom needed a ratio of one worker to two people, so we functioned mainly by relying on volunteers.

Mark turned up as a volunteer on a probation order – six-foot plus of seething rage, a frown permanently etched on his forehead and every other word unrepeatable in polite company. But when he worked with our clients, he was magically transformed; it was as if he took off a suit of armour. He was gentle, extraordinarily perceptive and responsive to people who couldn't communicate in the usual ways that others are able to understand. Above all, he oozed caring and compassion. Once the session was over, back on went the suit of armour.

Mark complained – a lot: this wasn't fair, that wasn't fair, life was hard, the world was cruel, his probation officer was an idiot (actually, the word he used is not printable), it was all the system's fault... I didn't know his story, but I could see his potential. I wondered what his life would look like if he took that suit of armour off permanently. At the end of a particularly hard session, back at the office, Mark was in full flow. Again. In a fit of madness probably driven by exhaustion, I pointed out that he should be grateful that his life didn't look like those of the people we worked with – which was really unfair. On a roll, I went on to suggest that he had potential way beyond anything that these poor folk could ever dream of, and if he didn't like the way the world looked he might consider shutting up, developing some of that potential and doing something about it. The office went quiet; I waited for the punch – actually, I was expecting at least two. They never came. Mark just looked at me, smiled and nodded gently. That was the beginning of an extraordinary thirty-year relationship between a young man from one of the toughest backgrounds imaginable and a middle-class public-school-educated idealistic hippy.

This is Mark's story of his journey. Being a part of this journey has been a privilege for me. It has helped me develop my own skills as a specialist mental health nurse for children, young people and their families, going on to specialise in working with parents experiencing difficulties in their relationships with their children, and then teaching on one of the largest professional nurse training programmes in the UK.

Mark's example has influenced my practice probably more deeply than any clinical guideline, literature review or randomised controlled trial – it has been a lesson in hopefulness, redemption and things turning out fine in the end, despite dreadful circumstances. He has become a part of my family, and he is my eldest daughter's godfather; she in turn is godmother to his eldest child.

If an angel had whispered in my ear in that first week of meeting Mark, 'This young criminal is going to be the chief executive officer of an award-winning group of therapeutic schools,' I might have suggested to the angel that they perhaps ease off on the drugs a little. Yet here we are. 'How does that even work?' you may ask. Read on, and you'll find out.

Fred Ehresmann,
Senior Lecturer in Mental Health Nursing,
University of the West of England

INTRODUCTION
My Story

My name is Mark Escott, and I'm the chief executive officer and co-founder of Life Chance Education, a therapeutic education provider that specialises in working with young people and families who have experienced trauma in their lives. I was one of them once, and I hope the story of my journey from victim to free agent, in control of my life and able to give something back, will persuade you that there is always hope.

In Part One, I explore how my own experiences led me to work in the area of education and social care and shaped my approach to it. Part Two covers the philosophy behind the schools I run, and looks at the challenges and triumphs of working successfully with vulnerable young people – successfully enough to have become the first school in the UK to achieve the Trauma and Mental-health-informed Schools Award.

The early years

On the day that I was born, my mum's mum died of cancer in another hospital some miles away. My mum was only nineteen, living in Devon, and she had met a man ten years older than her, who came from a council estate in Cardiff.

Shortly afterwards, we went to live with my nan and grandad in Cardiff. It wasn't a good move. My mum was mourning her mother, trying to look after a new baby and facing a lot of hostility as an Englishwoman living in Wales – not least, from my nan. To make matters worse, my dad was an alcoholic and a gambler, spending most of his time out of the house and leaving my mum on her own, with no money, struggling to keep me and herself fed.

It can't have been much of a life, so it's perhaps not surprising that when I was about two years old, she ran off with the next-door neighbour (who became my stepdad), taking me with her, back to Devon.

The first memory I have is of a supervised contact visit with my biological father, when I was about three years old. I went to the park with my dad and a social worker. When I was a little older, I had a conversation with my mum about that visit. I described how I remembered my dad, but it turned out that the man I was talking about was the social worker. I remembered him best because he had been kind to me. He had played with me in an effort to encourage my dad to do the same and to show him how to do it.

After the park, we went to a pub for lunch. I sat in the pub crying because I had always been told that I had to eat all my food. That wasn't a problem with the child portions that Mum served me, but here I was with an adult meal in front of me, scared that I was going to get shouted at for not being able to eat all of it.

Getting enough food for the family was a constant problem for my mum. By the time I was three and a half, there was another mouth to feed, as my sister had been born. My mum recalls having to count out and ration the slices of bread so that my sister and I could have our toast in the morning, and she would often go without food just so we children could have enough to eat. My wife was amazed when I told her that we would get an apple, a banana or a tangerine in our Christmas stocking. Fruit was so expensive that it was a rare treat.

I was always scared of my stepdad. He could be an angry man, and he often hit me. I soon learned that it was not good to cry, as he would hit me again, saying, 'Shut up, or I'll give you something to really cry about!' I also remember him not letting my mum comfort me in these times of distress.

My stepdad had encouraged me to deal with my dif-ferences with others by fighting. I'd seen him fighting with other men – on Christmas Day. He'd seen me getting beaten up by two boys as I went off to see a friend to show him one of my Christmas presents, and when I got back home he hit me for not having fought back hard enough. Then he went off to fight these boys' dads. I watched from the window, feeling traumatised by the whole experience.

There was often violence on the council estate where we lived. When I was about four or five, I witnessed the woman across the road having an argument with her boyfriend, and then stabbing him. We children fought a lot as well, and the police were always being called to the estate.

School

My school days were a nightmare. I couldn't read or write very well, but no one knew that I was dyslexic, so I got no special help. I was terrified of being shown up in class, and there was nothing worse than English lessons, when we'd have to read a page of a book out loud to the class. As my turn drew closer, I'd be thinking, 'I've got to get out of here; I've just got to get out of this room,' and then I'd do something silly like tip over a chair, punch the person next to me or swear at the teacher, because I knew that the teacher would probably drag me out of the classroom by the arm.

This was in the early 1970s, when physical punishment was acceptable at school. I remember being slapped on the hand with a ruler, hit with a board rubber and having my ears pulled. One teacher – let's call him Mr Hill – was an expert shot: when he threw a piece of chalk, he would hit you on the head every time. They wouldn't get away with any of that now!

They were always sending for my mum to come into the school to talk about my behaviour, which was really embarrassing for her. Then I was in trouble at home as well, and that meant some serious beatings. I remember my stepdad chasing me up the stairs, pulling me down by the leg and hitting me, using the familiar threat: 'I'll give you something to cry about!'

When I was about ten, my friend Phil and I decided to run away. He wasn't happy at home, I wasn't happy at home, and neither of us were looking forward to going to 'big school', where the work would be even harder. The plan was to go and live in the woods, so we took some food and clothes, and off we went. We walked for hours (or it felt like hours, anyway), but then we got scared and decided to go home. We got back to school at about lunchtime to find a huge commotion, kids pretending to film us as we walked back in, the police on site... and, of course, we were in bigger trouble than ever before.

Another thing that had a powerful impact on my life around this time – and one that I kept a secret for years – was that I had been groomed and sexually abused. Someone (I have never found out who) phoned the house when both my parents were at work and I was home alone. He asked me to touch myself sexually

9

and describe to him what it felt like. I felt powerless and went along with it. Afterwards, I was trapped: I couldn't tell anyone because he had threatened me, and I couldn't have stood the shame and humiliation of people finding out about it. Then, of course, I had to go along with his demands the next time he phoned, and the next...

He disappeared as suddenly as he had appeared, but even writing this now, after all these years, it turns my stomach. Thinking back to that time, I can see now that I craved any attention. And this is what hooked me into doing what he said. This soon turned into the guilt and shame that is commonly experienced by people like me, who have been abused. He used these emotions to manipulate me to carry on complying with his demands. After he disappeared, I was left with a toxic emotional legacy.

Reflecting on this period of my life, I realise that I was scared all the time: of the violence around me, of being shouted at, of being beaten and humiliated, but – most of all – of being shown up in front of my peers. This led me to explore ways of escaping from all the madness in my head.

Teenage years

I had my first cigarette and my first drink even before I was a teenager. I was ten or eleven when I first smoked, and I liked the rather woozy feeling it gave me. At the age of twelve, I started drinking. I felt woozy again, and realised that this was a way of blanking things out.

By the age of thirteen or fourteen I was sniffing glue. I wasn't going to lessons at school; I was skiving off with the glue that I had nicked from school to sniff. My friends and I had also learned that we could empty fire extinguishers and get a high from the gas left in them. And then I was introduced to cannabis.

It was at this point that I moved schools again. Here I was, a new boy from a rival town, getting into fights straight away to prove myself to all the people who were challenging me. When I wasn't being excluded or thrown out of classes, I was voting with my feet and walking out. It being a seaside town, I spent a lot of time in the arcades.

My new school tested me for dyslexia, and found that I was indeed dyslexic. Their solution? To place me in a class full of younger pupils who had also been diagnosed as dyslexic. It would have been just too embarrassing for me to go to this class.

Not that I was stupid: when I was given a multiple choice worksheet to do I worked out the pattern of the correct solutions, and they couldn't understand why I'd got all the answers right. When they put me on a computer, I hacked the system and completed the coursework assignment in a matter of minutes; they just couldn't figure out how.

My schooldays came to a sticky end when I was thrown out of the third and last exam I'd been entered for. Given that I was skiving off, smoking cannabis and had added magic mushrooms to the list of substances I was consuming, the signs weren't good. I turned up to the exam with a lump of cannabis and four cans of lager on me. The teacher found the lager in my bag and that was it. No exam.

I remember thinking that I was OK because they hadn't found the lump of cannabis in my trousers, and I went to the beach and got stoned. That was my memory of leaving school: getting kicked out on the last day for having lager. I was sixteen years old.

I left school with no GCSEs. I knew I was intelligent, but why couldn't I fit into the world I lived in?

Crime and punishment

All this time I'd been living with my mum, but when I was sixteen she kicked me out because of my violent behaviour, and I began sleeping on friends' sofas. I needed money, so I started committing crime and selling drugs. When I was seventeen I went to work at a holiday camp.

I worked in a kiosk selling sweets and cigarettes, as did another friend; another one worked as a cleaner. I made some friends who came from Moss Side, in Manchester, and I was able to get drugs through them. We used to take drugs at work, but we also teamed up to sell them, and we arranged parties and sold drugs at them too.

It was all going along fine until a few of my mates got tax rebates and decided to go to Spain to find work. My friend Simon and I wanted to go too, but we didn't have any money – we weren't great at not taking our stock of drugs, so we hadn't made much profit.

Simon, who was a couple of years older than me, suggested that the safe containing the takings from all the kiosks, which was kept in my kiosk, was the answer. We came up with a plan to steal the money and all the cigarettes stored in the kiosk so we could sell them. This wasn't such a big deal for me – I'd already done some robberies and some breaking and entering in the past.

We stole the money and the cigarettes, sold the cigarettes and got on a plane to Ireland so that Simon could see his mum, who he hadn't seen in over ten years. We had all this cash on us – eight or nine thousand pounds – and we headed to Dublin, to the estate where his mum lived. I remember being shocked that the shops consisted of metal cargo containers.

There was no reply at Simon's mum's flat, but her neighbours invited us in and gave us the sad news that she'd died two weeks before. A little digging around soon revealed a rumour that her boyfriend had dosed her with LSD and pushed her off a boat.

Simon then decided that we'd go and find this man. We were in Ireland with stolen money, we were on the run from the police, and we'd just found out how his mum had died. We then found out that Simon had relatives in a local fishing village, so we went off to search for them.

When we got there, we found Simon's grandma. She was delighted to see him, but other members of the family were not so delighted to see me. They took me to a ferry port, gave me fifty pounds (we'd already been robbed of the nine thousand pounds) and a punch in the head, and told me never to come back. I didn't argue; I got on the ferry from Dublin to Wales. By this time, I just wanted to get away from all this madness.

I got on the boat, petrified. I remember standing on the top rail of the ferry. I was thinking of jumping off, killing myself, when an Irishman stopped me from doing it – he pulled me down and took me for a beer. That was one of the darkest days of my life. My feelings of fear and despair are still clear in my memory.

Arrest and after

I arrived back in Wales. There was nowhere to go but my mum's, so I travelled down to Devon, where I was promptly arrested for the holiday camp robbery. This wasn't the first time I'd been arrested, but it was still pretty scary: I was thrown in a cell on my own, wondering what on earth it would be like if I went to prison for any length of time.

I got bail and stayed at my mum's house for a few weeks, until my case went to court. While I was waiting, I decided to visit my dad in Wales, who I hadn't seen since I was three years old. When I turned up on his doorstep, he'd just been discharged from hospital. They'd told him that if he carried on drinking, he would die. Of course, we met up and we went to the pub. It was just part of his routine: he'd have two raw eggs in a glass of brandy when he woke up, four cans of lager between 8am and 11am, and when the pubs opened he'd drink there for the rest of the day before going home to bed. Three months after our meeting, he was dead.

I went to the funeral, but I got some pretty negative comments from his friends and family. They were saying that I'd never cared about him and that I had left him. I was thinking, 'I was a baby when Mum left him, so how could that be my fault?' I phoned my aunty in Wales a couple of weeks later. My uncle answered the phone, and when I asked if I could talk to my aunty, I could hear him saying, 'What's that waste of space doing calling here?' The reaction from his family and their hostility towards me drove me take more drugs.

When my case finally came to court, I was given a two-year suspended sentence for theft and I was put on a two-year probation order. At that point, I was offered a room in a hostel for young men on probation.

By the time I went to live in the probation hostel, I was eighteen years old. There were five other young men in the hostel. Of those six of us, only two are still alive: my other friends there all died of drug overdoses or suicide.

Even on probation I was still involved in crime: I sold drugs, robbed a school for its computers, and even robbed a chemist for drugs.

The turning point

During this time, I was offered the chance to do some voluntary work at a drama and music project for young people with special needs. The thought of working with these kids scared me, but I didn't know quite why. I decided to go for it and do something completely different, something that would take me outside my comfort zone. Anything was going to be better than staring at the walls of the probation hostel every day for two years.

The project involved travelling to day centres to do drama and music activities with young adults who had a range of special needs. I found it was really fun: I enjoyed the caring side of the work, and I started to be able to identify myself as a carer. In my experience, people with special needs don't label you. They just accept you for who you are, what you are doing at that moment, how you're relating to them – and that's a rewarding thing.

I'd begun to give something back to society, and it made me realise that I didn't want to continue down the path of being a criminal.

And that's when I met Fred Ehresmann. Fred had just started his training as a mental health nurse, and he was working in the same drama and music therapy project where I was volunteering. He was involved with the project because he was also a talented musician. We got on well, and he took me under his wing. He even trusted me enough to invite me into his house. For the first time, I had an adult male in my life who believed in me and respected me. My self-esteem began to improve, and I met people who were doing some really interesting things.

Moving on

When I was coming to the end of my probation, one of my probation officers asked me what I wanted to do next. I told him that I wanted to do his job, because I thought he was shit. I told him that I wanted to be a translator, because 'I can learn your language, but you can never learn mine' – meaning that while I could learn all the jargon and theories of social work and probation, he would never be able to appreciate fully what it meant to have grown up with the life experiences that I had had. I said, 'You've never had any clue what it's like to be me. You've never understood me.' And I told him that I would go to college.

He answered that he didn't think I had the skills to do that. That's when Fred encouraged me to train for a national vocational qualification (NVQ) in community social care. He helped me with some of the course work, because I still couldn't read or write well. I found it a bit challenging and I didn't complete it, but just starting it gave me a real boost and got me on the path that led to the creation of Life Chance Education. In the end, the slight chip on the shoulder that the probation officer's attitude had given me spurred me on.

Looking back on this moment years later, I summed it up in the following statement:

> The first step of my career evolved from my experiences of living in a probation hostel in the 1990s. Coming to the end of my probation order, I was asked what I wanted to do next. I replied that I wanted to be a translator, someone who could erode the division between the language of the service user and the service provider.

I had never wanted to be the way that I was back then. I'd got trapped into a show of bravado, of pretending I was hard, of pretending I was tough – but it was all a lie. It took tremendous energy to keep up the façade that I was tough and hard and didn't give a shit. Inside I was still a scared little boy, but I had to try to pretend to be a man.

As soon as I started directing that energy outwards, things changed. When I stopped thinking about myself – because my lifestyle was selfish – and took up voluntary work, giving something back to other people, I began to see that I'd stopped being a victim. Other people had needs too.

I could now see the way forward, but that didn't mean that I would always keep to the path. As I began my career journey, I would see, time and again, how my experiences growing up had given me a unique insight into the struggles – and therefore the needs – of others whose early days had left them in a dark place.

PART ONE

LEARNING THE LANGUAGE

ONE

The Wounded Healer

When our wounds cease to be a source of shame
and become a source of healing, we have become
wounded healers.
– Henri Nouwen, Dutch
writer and theologian

Towards the end of my probation period, I heard someone talk about the concept of the 'wounded healer': someone who has been wounded by their own experiences, begins to ask themselves questions, and considers how they could put these experiences to good use. I started to look at how I, too, could take what had happened to me and use it to help others.

I recently typed the phrase 'wounded healer' into Google and found that it was coined by psychologist Carl Jung. I also discovered an enlightening piece of research related to this concept by psychotherapist Allison Barr. She sent a questionnaire to 253 psychotherapists and counsellors, and almost 74% of those who responded had had one or more wounding experiences in their lives that had led them to their chosen line of work.[1]

People make that choice because once they start to recover from these experiences, they realise that they can survive them and that, what's more, they have something to offer other people who are going through the same thing. In one sense, the professionals who surrounded me had only started their training at around the age of twenty. By that age, I already had twenty years' experience of what it was like to grow up in extremely disadvantaged circumstances. If people remark on how successful I've been in my career, I remind them that I've been developing expertise in it since the day I was born.

One clue to my resilience, despite all the poverty, crime and violence, is the fact that my mum always loved me. She might not have made the best of choices when it came to the men in our lives, but she has always been rock solid. Over the years, I have lost my freedom, lost friends, and even lost my mind to drugs, but Mum and I have never stopped loving each other.

---

1   A. Barr, 'An Investigation into the Extent to which Psychological Wounds Inspire Counsellors and Psychotherapists to Become Wounded Healers, the Significance of these Wounds on their Career Choice, the Causes of these Wounds and the Overall Significance of Demographic Factors' (The Green Rooms, 2006).

Onwards – and upwards?

By the age of twenty-one, I was starting to train as a drugs worker. Fred and I were now close friends, and he had even asked me to be his daughter's godfather. His wife, Annie, taught me to eat – and to cook – healthily. They and their friends were creative, went to festivals and wore bright clothes – I found it all very appealing. Fred also introduced me to meditation, healing and alternative therapies. I still do a lot of meditation now.

Another close friend of mine, Joanna Hollingbery, had helped me by letting me live with her. Jo is a philanthropist, and she also assisted me to set up my first charity. We become good friends over the years, and she is one of the people who helped to fund the schools I now run.

I was twenty-two when I set up a charity; it was called DANCE – Drugs and Narcotics Counselling and Education. We went to live music events and raves, giving out practical advice on how to keep safe while taking drugs; this was called the harm-minimisation approach. This stage of my career lasted for about two years, until the funding was cut and I moved on to other work in health and social care.

I became a support worker in a challenging-behaviour unit, helping young people in a residential setting. I found it easy to connect with them; I could build relationships with them quickly, because I could relate to their world. Of course, I was able to share some of my experiences with them – but even when I didn't, I think they could tell from the sort of person I was and how I behaved that I knew where they were coming from.

I started to train as a behaviour specialist, which gave me a much deeper understanding of the theories behind challenging behaviour. I also had to learn the practical aspects of dealing with it, so I trained in control and restraint techniques. Sometimes, with a colleague, I had to hold on to someone to stop them hurting themselves and others.

A childhood of training

The strange thing was, I found I wasn't afraid. Confronting someone who was getting violent didn't scare me – even when they were trying to lash out at me or kick me. I realised that I'd already been exposed to so much violence that I'd been desensitised to it. That meant I was able to stand in front of these people and communicate with them not just verbally, but through my body language. Somehow, I understood how to use a calm tone of voice and where best to position myself in the room.

When you're working in behaviour units, and in the schools that I've worked in since, you have to be good at reading the situation around you. Part of the training is in how to spot triggers in people's behaviour – you need to be aware of when they're getting anxious, when they're starting to get agitated and when they're getting angry, so you can intervene before they become violent.

All this came naturally to me. I had been reading danger in my own household and in the community from an early age. I'd been on the alert for violence from my stepdad, the teachers at school and the lads on the estates. I'd become adept at reading people's emotions and feelings.

The people who I was working with, and who were training me, began to acknowledge this, telling me I was really good at what I did. It dawned on me that I was a skilled behavioural specialist with a natural flair for getting into the world of my clients.

All the theories about challenging behaviour made perfect sense to me. I was taught that challenging behaviour is not the problem; it's the solution to a problem. When I heard that, I could relate it to my own life. That explained why I would behave so badly in class when we had to read aloud: the danger of being shown up in front of my schoolmates was such a huge problem that I could only solve it by acting up so that I'd get thrown out of the class. The teachers never realised that.

I'd found this way of coping, so I could understand when I saw others behaving in the same way. As a mentor had taught me, I could look behind the behaviour and appreciate that 'anger is just fear announced'. Just as I had been, many of these people were scared little boys. Once I realised that, it opened up a whole new conversation.

Really 'seeing'

Self-harm was another issue I had to deal with – one that people were often afraid to tackle. But this was how some of my friends had dealt with the distress caused by what was going on in their lives, and I too had cut myself to deal with all the pain I was feeling.

This deep understanding meant that I took a different approach when I talked to young people. I was able to acknowledge the meaning behind their behaviour. I'd say, 'I can see that you're self-harming and that you're using it to cope. I get that when you cut yourself, the pain that you feel takes you away from your situation and makes you numb to what's going on. So first of all, well done for having a go.'

They'd look at me in amazement, so I'd explain, 'I'm not condoning what you're doing, I'm just saying well done for trying to sort this out.' And that would open up a conversation about how this method was working out for them. Of course, it wouldn't be working out well, but then we could move on to a whole new dialogue. We could look at the things that were going on in their lives and how these things were affecting them, and I could start to use the coaching and counselling techniques that I'd been learning.

People would quickly open up to me, really talking – perhaps for the first time – about their experiences. They realised that I could really 'see' them. That was all I ever wanted when I was younger, that someone would 'see' me rather than just label me, and that was exactly what my clients wanted too.

By now I could see a career path for myself in social care, specifically in the field of challenging behaviour. I started working in the evenings at a youth club with young people aged twelve to eighteen who had just begun to experiment with drugs. I was searching for more opportunities too, but I was going to have to move away from Devon to find them.

The pendulum

I went to Brighton to work in a hostel dealing with people who displayed challenging behaviour. Some of them had mental health or drug and alcohol problems, and others were ex-offenders or on probation. It was similar to the hostel where I had lived in my teens.

There were a lot of different groups to deal with. Some were just children who were at the start of their criminal career, and I often felt they shouldn't be there. If they were homeless or things hadn't worked out at home, they ended up in the hostel, where they ended up learning plenty of skills that you wouldn't want them learning.

What they all had in common was bravado. I was frustrated by watching all these scared young men and women acting tough, and I was probably getting ideas above my station. I thought I could save the world. I thought that everyone would listen to me, because I was once one of them. But I was now an adult, and that meant they wouldn't listen to me.

I stayed at that hostel for four years, between the ages of twenty-five and twenty-nine. I was still growing up and growing in experience. The work was really challenging and I wasn't as successful at it as I wanted to be; so I started looking for ways to escape these feelings of failure. Just as I had done so many times before, I went into self-sabotage mode and got hooked on Brighton's party lifestyle. I started to use a lot of cocaine. I would do a twenty-four-hour shift or work long hours for three or four days in a row, and then I'd go and party hard.

I'd thought that quitting drugs and giving up crime was a one-way journey, but I was mistaken. Even when I was giving advice to other people about drugs, I was still leaning on drugs myself. It was as if I was on a giant pendulum: it seemed to be sweeping me forward to a better life, but just when I thought I'd cracked it, the pendulum would change direction and I'd end up going backwards.

Eventually, I became dependent on cocaine. I found myself starting to skip my work and ended up selling drugs so that I could ensure my own supply – but not on the scale of my old drug-dealer days. I just couldn't resist that backwards momentum; my demons seemed determined to hang on to me.

Sick and tired of being sick and tired

Somehow, I was able to live with the contradiction of being both drug advisor and drug addict – until I went to a party one night. I was taking coke, and I was off my head. Some people there asked me what I did, and I told them I worked in a hostel supporting other young people in the criminal justice system who were drug addicts and on probation. Then I told them a bit about my past, thinking they'd be impressed that I was a poacher turned gamekeeper. But they weren't impressed. They looked at me with disgust, and one of them said, 'That's outrageous: that you can still use drugs, be an addict, and think you can help these people. You're just a professional hypocrite.'

Hearing that word – hypocrite – shook my world. It made me take a close look at what I was doing. As I turned twenty-nine, I thought, 'I'm sick and tired of being sick and tired.' I decided that I would let go of the pendulum – not when it was on its backswing, when I would remain a drug user forever, but on the upswing, when I would be propelled into a career of working professionally as a practitioner.

The final push came when I went back to Devon to visit Fred. At the same time (don't ask me why), I went on a bender taking cocaine. I overdid it. I collapsed on the floor, but I managed to get to a phone and ring Fred. He came to the house and found me on the floor, fitting. Fred took me back to his house. I got some sleep, and when I woke up the next morning, Fred gave me his ultimatum.

'I can't cope with seeing you live like this any more,' he said. 'You've got too much potential. I love you, but you need to get your life started, and if you don't, I can't have anything else to do with you.' Apart from anything else, he wouldn't want to have me around his family. What sort of a godfather was I for his fourteen-year-old daughter?

The next day Fred took me to a meeting for people in recovery from drugs, and I joined the group. Over the next two months I relapsed a couple of times, but finally I broke free. I haven't done cocaine since I was twenty-nine.

I now know from my work as a behavioural therapist how hard it is to break a habit. They say it takes a hundred repetitions to learn a habit and up to a thousand to unlearn it. The approach of the recovery programme was total abstinence: I stopped taking cocaine; I stopped drinking alcohol. It was hard, but I had the underlying drive to pursue my career to keep me strong.

My recovery programme was powerful, but it wasn't enough. I talked in detail with Fred about the painful

events in my life, and he recommended having counselling as well. For the first time, I was able to take a
long hard look at my past without numbing myself to
the pain. I'd been suppressing a lot of this stuff and
dealing with my feelings of fear through drugs for
many years, but now I was facing life full on – looking
it in the eye and authentically feeling every emotion
that surfaced, however difficult that was. Sticking with
the counselling was certainly a challenge, but my future
was at stake.

A clean slate

The third strand of the recovery programme was working with a life coach, who was called Ellie Hale. I knew I
had something worth saying and sharing. I realised that
my own journey through education had been, to put it
bluntly, quite shit, but if education could be provided
differently, people like me could have a better start in
life. I told Ellie that I was going to commit myself to
working on transforming the education system.

'Brilliant!' Ellie said. 'But have you thought about how
you're going to do that? Let's look at this logically:
some of the things that you did in the past are still not
resolved. You may still be wanted by the police. How
are you going to have conversations with people in
the public arena with that hanging over you?' That's
when Ellie and I came up with the idea that I would
hand myself in to the police. By doing that, I could get
my integrity back.

About two weeks later, I walked to the local police station, went up to the desk and said to the duty officer, 'I want to hand myself in.'

'What for?' he asked.

'How long have you got?' I answered.

He looked at me as if I was absolutely crazy. 'Well, give me some idea.'

'Well, I've committed loads of crime since I was sixteen, I want to make a go of my future, and I want to talk to someone about what I've done.'

'OK, son, take a seat,' he said, and disappeared.

Twenty minutes later, a plain-clothes officer in a suit came out: a detective sergeant from the Criminal Investigation Department, or the CID. He took me into an interview room with another officer and got out a notepad, saying, 'Right, tell me what you're about.'

I told them a bit about my life story and about giving up drugs: that I was in recovery for cocaine addiction, that I was having life coaching and that I was committed to transforming the education system. I told them why I wanted to do it. They looked at me as if I was mad, but we filled three sheets of A4 paper with all the crimes I'd committed. When we'd finished, they said, 'OK, we're not quite sure what to do with this, but leave it with us. We take it that you're not a flight risk – you're not going to run away?'

A couple of times over the next two months they contacted me and asked me to come in and answer more questions about specific crimes I'd talked about. They asked me about some pub robberies that I'd mentioned and some car thefts in Birmingham. Then they let me go again.

All this time I was still working with my life coach. I was nervous about the whole police process, wondering what was going to happen. A month later, the local police asked me to come to a meeting with the chief constable at the police headquarters. I had to sit and wait outside his office with police officers all over the place, because the police headquarters was also where the police training college was.

The chief constable called me in, and I told him the story of why I had handed myself in and what I wanted to do. He then said to me, 'Well, I've looked at your crimes and we estimate that if we take them to court and prosecute you, you could go to prison for ten years. How do you feel about that?'

I told him that I was absolutely petrified of going to prison, but that I had to sort out my past; I was still committed to transforming the education system, so I would use my time in prison to study. And I told him that I saw myself as a poacher turned gamekeeper, so

I had lots of knowledge that I could share with young people. I believed I could help them turn their lives around.

Eventually, he said, 'I'm starting to understand that your word is important to you, isn't it? I think that you would be of more use to me in society doing the work that you want to do than you would be if I locked you up in prison, so I'm not going to prosecute you. But I want one thing from you.'

'What's that?' I asked.

'I want you to give me your word that you will fulfil your declaration that you will transform the education system and help other young people like yourself,' he answered.

At that point I felt complete; I no longer had to apologise for my past. I could put it all behind me and move forward. It was as if a great cloak of shame had been cut from my shoulders.

It had taken a long time, but at last I was ready to move on to the next phase of my life. Who was better qualified than me to prove that there are such things as second chances – many times over? 'Learning the language', and actually doing something with it, would mean a lot of hard work, though.

Key points

- The wounded healer has gained insights from their own experience that enable them to help others.

- The wounded healer can only help others effectively once they have healed their own wounds.

- All young people want to be 'seen', acknowledged and understood by another person.

- It takes many more repetitions to break a habit than to acquire one.

- Challenging behaviour must not be seen as the problem; it must be recognised as the young person's attempt to solve their problem at that time.

- Don't be fooled by bravado and aggression; anger is just fear announced – inside, the young person is lost and vulnerable.

TWO

Poacher Turned Gamekeeper

Labels are for filing. Labels are for clothing. Labels are not for people.
    – Martina Navratilova

Here I was: I'd made a commitment to the chief constable that I was going to transform education, and now I had to get on with fulfilling my promise. I'd wiped the slate clean and been given a second chance, free from the feelings of shame and unworthiness that had dogged my life so far. Now all I had to do was to get a job where I could start to use my skills and experience, and really make an impact.

The behaviour mentor project

At the time I was sharing a flat with a friend who worked in a school. He introduced me to an advanced skills teacher called Kate Scarlett, who specialised in

behaviour management. She worked with her colleague Phil Gasson, who also specialised in this area.
Their jobs involved training other teachers to handle
challenging behaviour in the classroom. One evening
I was talking to them about my experiences, both in
my childhood and in working with young people. Two
days later Kate phoned me up, all excited, to tell me
about a new position that had opened up at her school.

It was a secondary school in Devon that also provided
specialist training for teachers, and they wanted someone to set up and run a pilot behaviour mentor project
in the school. The aim of the project was to tackle any
problems that were preventing students from learning, such as emotional and behavioural difficulties,
family breakdown, drugs and alcohol, and bullying.
They wanted to bring someone with a youth work and
social care background into an education setting for
the project. It fitted perfectly with what I'd been doing
over the last ten years. I applied for the post and got
selected for interview.

When I went along for the interview, it was the first
time I'd been inside a school since I'd been kicked
out just before my last exam. It looked like a school, it
felt like a school – it even smelt like a school – and it
reminded me of my own school. All these emotions
started welling up in me. 'What am I doing here?' I
thought. My internal commentary was telling me to
get the hell out, because any minute now I was going
to be unmasked as a fraud.

I was one of a group of ten interviewees. There were three stages to the interview: as well as a formal session with the interview panel, we had to meet the students and give them a presentation, and take part in a role-play. I noticed that some of the candidates found meeting the pupils difficult. They'd come back into the waiting area saying things like, 'Those children are really hard to engage; they're just not interested.'

I then went in and began a presentation about what they wanted to do when they left school. Sadly, some of them told me they weren't bright enough to pass exams and get jobs. We then moved on to talking about travelling. They asked me if I had travelled, so I told them about my journeys to India, Egypt, Thailand and all across Europe. I ended up having an amazing conversation with them. They were full of life, and the person overseeing the assessment said, 'I've never seen them engage with anyone like that before.' That made me feel really good.

The next stage was a role-play session in which two drama teachers and one of their students played the parts of two parents and their child meeting me, the school's behaviour manager. The father was aggressive towards the mother, shouting at her and at the boy, and it was obvious that there was domestic violence in the family. The drama teachers played their parts so convincingly that one of the interviewees left the room in tears.

Perhaps because of my own background I'd become desensitised to such situations. For whatever reason, I'd become pretty confident at dealing with these encounters, and I shone at this part of the assessment. I realised I'd actually enjoyed the whole process.

The next day, they called me to say I'd got the job. I stayed at that school for three and a half years, setting up a behaviour support centre to merge education and social care in the school, and doing a lot of other things besides, including helping to write the school's behaviour, drugs and anti-bullying policies. I worked with young people individually, but also set up groups for them. Because it was a training establishment, I also began to train teachers in emotional intelligence, child brain development and neuroscience, which I was passionate about at the time.

A GAP IN TEACHER TRAINING

When I started talking to the teachers about brain development and how we learn, I said to them, 'I don't want to be patronising or try to teach my grandmother to suck eggs, but...' One them asked, 'Why are you saying that?' When I answered that it was because I assumed that they knew much of this already, as they must have covered it in their training, I turned out to be completely wrong. Back in 2002, the science behind brain development wasn't on the agenda for teacher training like it is today. This was when I truly understood that social care, health and education needed to be far more closely dovetailed.

Clearly, much of the knowledge that people who worked in social care and mental health services possessed wasn't being shared with schools. This insight planted a seed about how I was going to transform the education system. What's more, I realised that I was becoming fluent in all three languages: education, health and social care.

Focus on mental health

After three and a half years, I left the school in Devon and went to set up a similar project at a school in Bristol. During this time I was approached by Shoba Manro, the manager of the local Child and Adolescent Mental Health Services (CAMHS) team, which is a branch of the NHS. Shoba was a dynamic and innovative leader with a background in social services, so appointing her to manage a CAMHS team was an unusual move.

Shoba wanted to create two one-year secondments to bring a behaviour specialist from the education field and a social worker into the team. I was given the behaviour specialist post, working alongside Jon Simons, who'd been appointed to the social work post.

Being in this new CAMHS team was great, but it took time for the other NHS staff to accept us. They didn't quite 'get' us. As we hadn't come through the ranks of the NHS as they had, we weren't part of the old boys' (and girls') network.

ARE THEY FOR REAL?

When I was experimenting with drugs as a teenager, my mum took me to our GP because she couldn't understand my mood swings. The GP referred me to the local CAMHS team. On our way to the appointment, on the third floor at the clinic, I noticed that there was netting in the stairwells – a safety measure in case anyone took it into their head to jump. 'So they actually think I'm mad,' I thought. At this point I realised: do not tell these people anything in case they label you as mad and lock you up. Go in, say as little as possible, get out.

Years later, at the interview for my secondment to a CAMHS team, the panel was made up of therapists, doctors and so on. They asked the usual questions about why I wanted to work with them, and I had no difficulty in answering them. But at the end of the interview, I went up to some of the doctors and touched them on the hand. 'Why are you doing that?' they asked. I told them that I'd not been in a room with professionals like them since I was a teenager. I'd heard about them a lot on my journey so far, and now here they were again. In the flesh. But this time, I was the professional too. Was it all a dream?

After my year on secondment, a job came up that involved me training as a primary mental health specialist – that's 'primary' in the sense of a first point of contact for health care rather than anything to do with primary schools. The role of the primary mental health specialist is to be the link between universal first contact services for children and families, known as Tier One services, and the specialist service that is

CAMHS. It meant working with frontline services like schools, and developing teachers' and other professionals' knowledge about mental health.

I'd visit social services teams and schools, working with individual students as a consultant. I'd also assess what the professionals' needs were and create training packages for social services and teachers about children's mental health and wellbeing. I ran training sessions, provided consultancy and supervision, and sometimes coached staff. I worked right across the sector, with health, social care, education, the youth justice system and non-statutory providers (such as charities, social enterprises and other not-for-profit organisations).

Part of my work also involved promoting the emotional health of children, young people, families and carers in the community. I supported primary and secondary education too, working alongside social services. I spent four years with this team, training and working as a primary mental health specialist.

I loved being in this broad role, because I started to gain some valuable insights into the people who were responsible for taking care of me when I was a child. For example, when I was running the parent support programmes, the sessions took place in a contact centre. The centre reminded me of the contact visit I had had with my dad under the supervision of the social worker, and the feelings came flooding back. This sort of environment just didn't work for me: these places certainly didn't feel welcoming.

THEY'RE STILL MY FAMILY

At a 'Team Around the Child' meeting, I was sitting with a clinical psychologist, a psychiatrist, a family practitioner, a social worker and a youth worker before the parent and child arrived. I think it was the psychiatrist who said, 'It's not surprising they've been referred to us, because they are so dysfunctional.'

I had to say something: 'Look, I'm from that world. My family would have been called dysfunctional, but as a child I didn't know they were dysfunctional. All I knew was that they were my family and I loved them.' I continued, 'I just want to put that into the arena because I think that sometimes gets lost. We're looking at them as a dysfunctional family, but we have to understand that this is all they know. This is intergenerational; it's been going on in families for years. If we take that approach, rather than automatically putting them in the wrong and labelling them, we might be able to get into their world a bit more.'

The psychiatrist dismissed my comments and was a bit rude because I'd challenged him. One of the other professionals at the meeting told me that it wasn't my place to challenge the consultant. I just told him that I thought I had a right to share my opinion.

Connecting with families

In this role, I had many opportunities to observe highly qualified professionals at work. I witnessed a consultant assessing a child for ADHD. He had a wealth of knowledge and was asking a lot of questions, but I was listening to what the child's mum had to say. I was in awe of the doctor, and I could see that the mother was too. I could sense that the answers she was giving were what she felt the psychiatrist wanted to hear; she wasn't sharing information authentically. The child himself wasn't saying a lot because he was in a strange environment.

I was surprised by how short the assessment was. It dawned on me that because all assessments are based on the information given by the clients, if you're not creating an environment where people can be honest with you, you're never going to arrive at a full and authentic assessment.

I had been labelled as ADHD as a child, and I'd worked with lots of children with different labels. I'd already started to become too attached to listening to the labels and not meeting the individuals. I realised that I had never actually met ADHD. It had never walked into my clinic and said, 'Hello, I'm ADHD. Little Johnny is just getting out of the car and he'll be with us in a minute.'

I started to see that difficult and challenging behaviour in young people exists on a continuum of the impact on the young person and the people around them. At one end of the scale is behaviour that might be difficult for one adult to manage but simply puzzling or irritating for another. At the other end of the scale is behaviour that unquestionably generates feelings of frustration, anxiety, distress and anger for everyone. These difficulties cause the most concern for school staff, who

ONE MORE LIFE CHANCE

may wonder whether the child has been (or should be) diagnosed with a specific condition.

Many of the young people I had come into contact with had been diagnosed with a specific disorder. Although you have to be careful when making direct causal links between the diagnosis and particular behaviours, the presence of a diagnosis can allow you to make some broad and useful assumptions.

Take the child I sat in the room with, for example. If a young person has been diagnosed as having ADHD, they probably have a history of difficulties with restlessness, over-activity, poor concentration, impulsiveness and being unable to wait their turn in games and conversations. This might have affected their friendships, school and home life, along with their self-esteem and their view of the world. A diagnostic label will point to the presence of certain limitations and needs for the young person, which may be linked to your concerns about their behaviour. This will alert you to the need for care in how you understand and respond to the young person.

It's usually easy to find general information about a diagnosis, and there may also be suggested strategies and general principles for working with a young person who has that diagnosis. But this information will be of limited use when dealing with individual situations that need tailored responses. There's no substitute for getting to know someone and finding out about their own strengths and difficulties, regardless of whether they have a diagnosis.

Communicating through emotional intelligence

Let's face it, the only experts in the room who really know the child are the child and their parent or carer, so it pays to listen to them carefully.

I realised this because of my life journey and the training I'd had in my career so far. I had developed a higher level of emotional intelligence. Emotional intelligence is how you shape your thoughts and feelings, how you communicate them to others, and how you respond to the emotions expressed by others.

Although I had been sitting on the same side of the table as the doctor, I knew exactly how it felt to be sitting on the opposite side, with the mother and her son. I could see how his identity could become swallowed up by the ADHD diagnosis. Although he might *have* ADHD, it wasn't right to say he *was* ADHD. How could you hope to get inside his world if he had been completely swallowed up by his diagnosis?

Becoming a translator

Working across so many different areas, I began to understand how different the languages of social care, health and education really were. To give just one example, when I began to talk to teachers about supervision and coaching, they were taken aback, thinking that they'd done something wrong. But in mental health and social care, these are standard therapeutic practices: everyone acknowledges that this work is emotionally demanding and that you need to be able to talk your experiences through with a senior practitioner to get their advice, reassurance and support. It's an important part of helping you develop your practice and improve how you interact with your clients.

Uncovering teachers' mistrust of supervision and coaching enabled me to navigate conversations with them and present my training in ways they found acceptable. Since then, education has taken a massive leap forward and teachers have taken on a lot more responsibility for looking after children's wellbeing and safety. The veils between education, social care and health have been getting thinner and thinner.

It was fascinating to master the languages of all three disciplines: social care, health and education. I was fulfilling the ambition I'd expressed all those years ago – of becoming a translator, of being able to pull together all those strands for the benefit of parents and children.

Advanced skills

I was always on the lookout for opportunities to hone my skills, and freelance work as an independent panel member for a foster care company allowed me to do just that. I was part of a team that was responsible for screening applications from people who wanted to be foster carers. The applicants had to go through an intensive interview process that lasted for several months. They had to reflect on their own lives, explain why they wanted to be foster carers, and give information about their backgrounds, who else lived in their house, and so on. This was written up and given to us panel members to weigh up. Then we interviewed the candidates and made the final decision on whether they could be employed by the foster care company.

I also wanted to come home to Devon again, and eventually I left the CAMHS team to do so. I wanted to start working in my own community – giving something back to other young people like myself. When I first moved back, I spent some time working as a freelance child-behaviour specialist, delivering training, coaching and consultancy to schools in Devon and Cornwall on behaviour management in the classroom and looking at child brain development, neuroscience and emotional intelligence.

Growing awareness

As a freelance worker, I missed the support of working in a team. So I got a job as an advisory teacher in a behaviour support team, providing outreach, coaching, advice, support and training to primary and secondary schools to help them meet the needs of children with social, emotional and mental health difficulties.

I travelled round to many different schools, met lots of staff – teachers, learning support assistants, senior leaders, deputy heads, head teachers – and worked with them to improve the emotional wellbeing and behaviour of the children in their school. I'd do assessments of children and then coach the staff on how to engage with these children.

I began to see that many children were not able to fit into mainstream school, for a variety of reasons:

- Sensory processing disorders

- Mental health difficulties

- Attachment disorder

My job was to keep children in school – inclusion – but I started to realise that this wasn't appropriate for some of these children, because the schools weren't designed to support them: one size doesn't fit all. Many of the staff members I worked with were struggling. They were amazing people, but they were in a situation where they were pedalling fast all the time without getting anywhere. They didn't have the time or the resources.

Meanwhile, these children were slipping through the net, and the more able children were failing to make progress because such a large part of school resources was being diverted to children with these particular needs. My research continued to highlight increasing numbers of exclusions of students who were finding it difficult to fit in to existing education provision. It became clearer that one of the largest obstacles to these young people's learning was the trauma they had experienced in their lives. This was affecting not only their education but also their social and emotional development. I realised that if I wanted to fulfil my promise to transform the education system, I would need to concentrate on working with young people who had experienced trauma in their lives, and I would need to do a lot more research in this area.

Around this time, I came across the phrase 'adverse childhood experiences' (ACEs). In the next chapter we'll take a closer look at the variety of experiences that can be described as ACEs. I'll explain why it was such an important next step in my career and played such a huge part in my own healing.

Key points

- Labelling stands in the way of understanding a child fully and being able to engage with them.

- Anyone involved in social care or therapy needs to be able to read (and listen) between the lines, read the signs, and be sure that they aren't just getting the answers that their client thinks they want to hear.

- Children don't know their families are dysfunctional; for the most part they just love their family, no matter how difficult the circumstances.

- Teachers' pastoral responsibilities mean that they are now as much in need of supervision and coaching as those who work in social care.

- A 'one size fits all' approach in mainstream schools means that children with particular needs are at risk of slipping through the net.

- A therapeutic education model provides hope for children who cannot cope in mainstream provision, and relieves pressure on teacher time and school resources.

THREE

Adverse Childhood Experiences

Give me a child until the age of seven, and I will
show you the man.
  – Aristotle

My research into childhood trauma revealed some
interesting – yet devastating – information.
Everything I learned confirmed my own experiences,
both from my own childhood and from the countless
children and young people I had met in my career. In
this chapter we'll look in detail at the main research
into this area, which underpins my philosophy of Life
Chance Education.

What are ACEs?

ACEs is an acronym for 'adverse childhood experiences'. It describes a wide range of stressful or traumatic experiences that children can be exposed to while they are growing up. These range from experiences that directly harm a child (such as suffering physical, verbal or sexual abuse, or physical or emotional neglect) to those that affect the environment in which a child grows up (including parental separation, domestic violence, mental illness, alcohol abuse, drug use or imprisonment). Childhood experiences, both positive and negative, have a tremendous impact on whether someone will be a perpetrator or victim of violence in the future, and, more broadly, on their health and opportunities in life.

When I first came across the concept of ACEs, I had a flashback to my own childhood. It was like being on a roller-coaster ride through different times in my life: the first memory of my dad and that supervised contact visit with him, seeing my neighbour being stabbed by his girlfriend, my own experience of physical and emotional abuse, my descent into drug and alcohol misuse, and my arrest and detention in my teens. I had to find out more.

The ACEs study

The first ever ACEs study was part of the biggest public health study ever conducted in the United States. Led by Dr Vincent Felitti and Dr Robert Anda, the study was a collaboration between the Centers for Disease Control and Prevention and the integrated managed care consortium Kaiser Permanente's Preventive Medicine Department. As part of the project, 17,000 people were questioned about their health history and childhood experiences.[1] The researchers found a direct link between ACEs and poor mental and physical health decades later – and, in some cases, early death. A phenomenon known as toxic stress was the key to the negative effects of ACEs.

ACEs and toxic stress

Stress is a physiological response to an adverse event or challenging circumstance, and it causes biochemical changes in our bodies. There are three recognised types of stress.

- **Positive stress** is a normal response to mildly challenging situations that happen from time to time, and all children need to experience it to grow and develop in a healthy way.

- **Tolerable stress** results from more severe, frequent or sustained adverse experiences, but it causes no lasting damage as long as the child enjoys nurturing

---

1   V.J. Felitti, R.F. Anda, D. Nordenberg, D.F. Williamson, A.M. Spitz, V. Edwards, M.P. Koss, and J.S. Marks, 'Relationship of Childhood Abuse and Household Dysfunction to Many of the Leading Causes of Death in Adults', *American Journal of Preventive Medicine*, 14/4 (1998), 245–58.

relationships and is provided with consistent emotional support. These relationships and this support constitute a buffering effect, which prevents ongoing harm.

- **Toxic stress** occurs when the body's stress response is triggered by an intense experience that is often repeated and sustained. Without the buffering provided by caring, supportive adults, this severe type of stress can cause permanent and significant damage to brain development. It is particularly damaging when the toxic stress occurs in the key years of child development and growth.

Experiences that are typically damaging for a child during development include severe physical or emotional abuse and chronic neglect.

Again, the term 'toxic stress' really hit home. 'Toxic' was exactly the word I would use to describe the world I had grown up in. I could clearly see the intergenerational impact of this toxic stress: it had been affecting us as a family over and over again.

Types of ACEs

The original study of ACEs looked at ten ACEs across three main categories:

Abuse

- Physical abuse
- Sexual abuse
- Emotional abuse

Neglect

- Physical neglect
- Emotional neglect

Family circumstances

- Domestic violence
- Substance abuse (including alcohol)
- Mental illness
- Parental separation and divorce
- Parental imprisonment

Since then, more adverse experiences have been identified and added to the list:

- Being bullied or experiencing discrimination
- Witnessing a sibling being bullied or abused
- Seeing someone threatened or attacked with a gun or knife

- Having to leave one's home or country because it wasn't safe

- Living in an unsafe neighbourhood

- Being extremely ill or injured, or a family member being ill or injured

- Being taken into foster care

- Losing a loved one

- Moving home or school repeatedly

WITNESSING PARENTAL VIOLENCE

A small child can be traumatised by witnessing domestic violence. Usually, a child will look at their mother when hearing her voice, which helps the child to build a stronger attachment and develop relationship skills. But seeing a parent being physically attacked is so distressing that the child will look away whenever an attack begins to happen. If the mother experiences domestic violence repeatedly, the child may be unable to look at her in case they see her being attacked. This reluctance to make eye contact may lead to difficulties in communicating and establishing relationships later in life.

Throughout my career I have worked with many young people in care and seen first-hand what it's like for them to keep moving from one carer and home to another. I also know how it felt not to have seen my dad throughout my childhood. With that in mind, I would add three more ACEs to this list:

- Multiple changes or breakdowns in carer (including foster carer) placements

- Being placed in a residential home (lack of physical touch)

- Sporadic or inconsistent contact with a parent

The impact of ACEs

The more ACEs a child experiences, the higher their risk of physical illness. The range of conditions that can be traced back to ACEs includes:

- Heart attacks

- Strokes

- Cancer

- Diabetes

- Chronic lung disease

- Autoimmune disease

- Sleep disturbances

- Eating disorders

- Headaches

- Obesity

- Asthma

- Irritable bowel syndrome

- Early death

ACEs are implicated in the ten leading causes of death in the western world.[2]

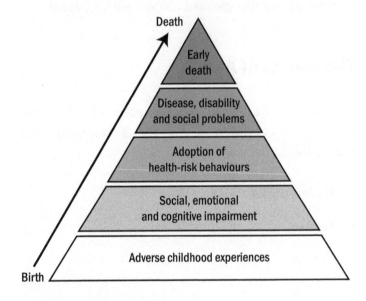

Figure 3.1 The ACEs pyramid

As the number of ACEs experienced by a person increases, so does their risk of mental illness and attachment issues, including:

2   M. Burt, 'What Will it Take to End Homelessness?' (Washington DC: Urban Institute, 2001), http://webarchive.urban.org/publications /310305.html.

- Depression

- Anxiety

- Behaviour disorders

- Addiction to drugs, alcohol or smoking

- Learning difficulties

- ADHD

- Violent behaviour

- Domestic violence

The wider consequences for the person are equally negative:

- Unemployment

- Poor educational attainment

- Teenage pregnancy and parenthood

- Troubled relationships

- Attempted suicide

The cumulative effect of ACEs

The impact of one ACE can be severe, but sadly many people experience multiple ACEs during their childhood, and it's not hard to see how one ACE might lead to another (domestic violence being the cause of parental separation, for example). The following table shows the cumulative impact of multiple ACEs:

No ACEs	Three or more ACEs	Four or more ACEs
Most children (97%) have no learning difficulties	Children are three times as likely to experience academic failure, five times as likely to have attendance problems, and six times as likely to have behaviour difficulties	Half of children have learning difficulties, and they are thirty-two times more likely to have behaviour difficulties

With each additional ACE, there is a higher risk of:

- learning difficulties

- behaviour difficulties

- becoming a serious violent offender by the age of thirty-five

Health consequences

The original ACEs study focused on how ACEs have affected health in adults, and so has much of the work done since. These health problems, including early death, often result from health-risk behaviours (see the top three layers of the ACE pyramid). The psychological impact of living with toxic stress can lead to a person behaving in a way that seems to take the pain away, but actually harms their health:

- Smoking

- Alcohol abuse

• Drug abuse

• Sex addiction

• Self-harm

The neurological impact of living with toxic stress can damage the structure and functions of the body and the brain, in particular:[3] Neurochemical systems (the chemical processes of the nervous system):

• Neuroanatomy (the anatomy of the nervous system)

• Endocrine system (glands in the body that control the metabolism)

• Immune system

• Autonomic nervous system (the part of the nervous system that controls bodily functions that are not consciously directed, such as breathing)

TOXIC STRESS AND CORTISOL

Cortisol is the body's response to fear and stress. Released by the adrenal glands, it prepares us for the 'fight or flight' response. We can observe this in action through, for example, elevated heart and breathing rates and dilated pupils. Cortisol is important for keeping us safe in certain situations, but without the neurochemicals that break

---

3   N. Burke Harris, N (2014), 'How Childhood Trauma Affects Health Across a Lifetime' [video], (TED talk, 2014), www.ted.com /talks/nadine_burke_harris_how_childhood_trauma_affects_health _across_a_lifetime?language=en

cortisol down, it can build up to toxic levels that can damage children's language development, empathy, impulse control, mood regulation, short-term memory and the connections between sensory experiences and how they are feeling. Over time, this can affect how they develop social relationships and a sense of self, and their ability to concentrate and learn. The brain is a social organ: it develops in response to input from those around it. That means the brains of the adults around a child's developing brain – and how these adults use their brains – will have a major impact. Stressed-out brains produce more stressed-out brains (see the diagram 'Formation of a secondary trauma').

Intervening early

At Life Chance Education, when we work with children and young people who have experienced ACEs, we focus on the lowest two layers of the ACEs pyramid. Working at this level during the childhood and teenage years can prevent the onset of the problems in the highest three layers.

Children who have suffered multiple ACEs will display significant social, emotional and mental health difficulties, as well as learning difficulties, because their cognitive functions have been damaged by their exposure to ACEs.

- **Social difficulties** include the inability to form or maintain relationships, to communicate their feelings, and tolerate the opinions and needs of others.

- **Emotional difficulties** include extreme difficulty in regulating their emotions, recognising their triggers, developing strategies to control their own behaviour, and hyperarousal (this occurs when a person's body is triggered into high alert as a result of thinking about their trauma. Even though the real danger may not be present, the body reacts as if it's in the same danger as after a traumatic event).

This developmental trauma also affects a person's 'executive functions': their ability to organise, problem-solve, move from one activity to another, maintain attention and so on.

THE BRAIN – A SOCIAL ORGAN

The brain is a social organ. Although it matures by around the age of twenty-five, it has the capacity to rewire itself constantly throughout life. This is known as 'neuroplasticity'. Although ACEs and toxic stress can have a negative effect on a child's development, if they have consistently positive experiences with emotionally available adults, their brain's neuroplasticity can play a central role in the healing process – a biological basis for hope. This can only really happen if these adults receive the care and attention that they need to weather the emotional storms of supporting children who have experienced childhood trauma. Secondary trauma in these adults creates a vicious cycle as the children, trapped in their experiences of trauma, affect those who seek to help them. Stressed-out brains create stressed-out brains.

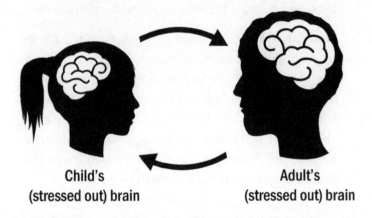

Child's
(stressed out) brain

Adult's
(stressed out) brain

Figure 3.2 Formation of secondary trauma[4]

Knowing about a student's ACEs and when they occurred allows a school to consider the extent to which the development of these crucial functions has been affected. In turn, this allows the school to pitch the academic curriculum at the correct level, not expecting a child to make progress in English and Maths if they haven't first developed the ability to organise themselves, use their working memory or shift from one activity to another.

At Life Chance Education's therapeutic day schools, the School for Inspiring Talents and the ACE Clinic, the work concentrates on the impact of the childhood

---

4   Center on the Developing Child at Harvard University (2011), 'Toxic Stress Derails Health Development' [video] (2011), https://developingchild.harvard.edu/resources/toxic-stress-derails-healthy-development

trauma that has led to these young people being excluded, or being in danger of being excluded, from mainstream education settings. This work is underpinned by a clear understanding of which ACEs the child or young person has experienced and at what stage in their development. Only in this way it is really possible to help children and young people recover from their early trauma and develop all the skills and emotions needed to lead a happy, healthy and fulfilling life as they get older.

A large part of developing Life Chance Education, the School for Inspiring Talents and the ACE Clinic came from discussions I had with my mum. We talked about what would have been helpful for both of us as we tried to navigate our own life experiences. The development of my career has in fact been a healing process for both of us. We get such joy from being with my own children, who have the amazing opportunity to break the intergenerational cycle of toxic stress in our family and transform the life chances of the generations to come.

Key points

- There is a direct link between ACEs and poor mental and physical health decades later.

- The toxic stress that intense and repeated ACEs inflict on the body can cause permanent and significant damage to brain development, especially if it occurs in the key years of child development and growth.

- Types of ACEs fall broadly into three categories: abuse, neglect and family circumstances.

- Children who have experienced three or more ACEs are six times more likely to develop behaviour difficulties than children with no ACEs.

- An academic school curriculum is not suitable for children who haven't developed the ability to organise themselves, concentrate or move from one activity to another.

- Toxic stress is contagious because the brain is a social organ: those working for long periods of time with children and young people experiencing trauma are at risk of becoming traumatised themselves, so it's important that staff get regular supervision.

PART TWO
TRANSFORMATIONS

FOUR
Setting Up Life Chance Education

I'm not afraid of storms, for I'm learning how to sail my ship.
    – Louisa May Alcott

A new model

If you've read the previous chapter on ACEs, you can imagine how enlightening all this information was for me. While I was still working as an advisory teacher and researching more and more about trauma and ACEs, I was approached by a couple of colleagues, David Strudwick and Judith Johnson. They talked about setting up a specialist school to work with children who were slipping through the net. We knew there was a big gap between the two sorts of provision that existed at the time. At one end of the scale there were special schools for children with a range of emotional issues, schools for children with physical disabilities and schools for children with learning difficulties. At the other end of the scale there were pupil-referral units, or alternative provision for, stereotypically, children 'with challenging behaviour'.

If we could create a hybrid between the two, taking best practice from health, social care and education, and blending it in a school setting, we could create something unique and innovative.

When I'd been working in the CAMHS team under Shoba Manro, it had moved to new premises in a recently opened school. The school had been renting out vacant space until it had achieved its full intake, and for me it had made the perfect location for the CAMHS team (though not everyone agreed). During lunchtimes, I'd been able to have conversations with the special educational needs staff, other teachers or the head teacher, and we had shared useful and constructive knowledge.

I said to Dave and Judith, 'When I worked in CAMHS, we were based in a school for eighteen months. Wouldn't it be great to have a CAMHS school?' It was because of this that we began looking into opening a therapeutic school. We tried to set up our school as a free school under the government's new scheme. The school was to be called the School for Inspiring Talents.

In the end we were unsuccessful, because we didn't fit into anyone's boxes. They were asking, 'Are you a mainstream school, a specialist school or alternative provision?' We were a hybrid between alternative provision and a special school, but it was really hard to get this message across. Dave left the project to be involved in setting up another free school, which left me and Judith. At this stage, Judith and I decided to expand on the idea of our School for Inspiring Talents.

In discussing my own past with Judith – the work that I'd been doing since my teens, and all that I'd learned – we realised that I had in fact been given another life chance. That's how the concept of our company, Life Chance Education, came about. We decided to set it up as a private school. I made the decision to leave my job, and my last day as an advisory teacher was on 31 March 2014.

On 1 April 2014 (April Fool's Day – was fate trying to tell me something?) I dedicated myself to working full time on setting up the Life Chance Education company and its first school, the School for Inspiring Talents.

From flipchart to policy

When I first saw the application form from the Department for Education, I thought it was pretty scary and unbelievably complex. But then, I realised that that was exactly as it should be. They couldn't have just anyone setting up a school on a whim, could they? It made me wake up to the size of the task I was taking on – the degree of responsibility that would be on my shoulders. It was not a thing to be taken lightly.

I started filling out the easy bits: who Judith and I were, as proprietors of the school; where it would be situated (I was going through the process of looking for premises at the time); and what it would be called. The next bit asked me to outline the school's policies on safeguarding, health and safety, and attendance – not so easy.

After that, the form asked me to set out short-term, mid-term and long-term lesson plans, describe the ethos of the school, specify where we would get our referrals from, and give details of how it would be funded.

We weren't eligible for the sorts of grants that were on offer to people who were setting up free schools, so we had to set up as an independent private school and raise funds to do this. I approached my friend Joanna Hollingbery, the philanthropist. Though Jo thought the company was a great idea, she didn't want to invest in it – but she said she might lend us the money to set it up. She sent me one of her business advisors, James Arnold Baker, to look at the school's business plan. He reported back to her that he thought it was a good business model and that he believed it would be successful, enabling me to pay back a loan in the not-too-distant future. As a result, Jo gave us an interest-free loan. Jo also played an important part in making the idea of the school a reality. She even volunteered in the school during its first week of opening.

James Arnold Baker became like a mentor to me, helping me to understand how to run the business side of the school. In acknowledgement of the huge part he played before his death in 2018 I named one of my new school buildings after him.

To map out all that I needed to do, I started writing down on flipchart paper everything that the form asked for. Every day I would add more items: all the policies that were needed, all the additional research that was needed. Every time I completed a task, I crossed it off my list, but I often needed to add another item in its place. At the height of this process, the walls of my dining room were covered with flipchart paper – it was all-encompassing, but it had to be done. It took a couple of months, but by the end of it we had found premises and got the builders in to convert them into a school.

The first thing I asked the builders to do was to complete my office; then at least I could take my flipchart paper down there and plaster it all over the walls. One by one I took the sheets down as real policies, real systems – a real school – took shape. One by one, new rooms in the school came 'on stream' as they were completed and fitted out ready for their purpose. Eventually, there was only one more hurdle to get over.

The Ofsted acid test

Before the school could open, it had to be inspected by Ofsted (the government's Office for Standards in Education). I had to get the school completely ready to take in students before I could get the Ofsted inspector to come and do a pre-registration inspection, and either pass or fail the school for opening. On the day, all the furniture was in the school, there were displays on the wall and teachers on the payroll, and every policy and procedure that the Department for Education had asked for was arranged neatly in binders and files laid out on the table for scrutiny.

This was the scariest bit of all: I had borrowed – and spent – all this money, put in all this time, and here was a fully functioning school in front of me, but I was waiting on one person to tell me whether it was good enough to open or not. And with perfect timing, my wife had chosen the night before the inspection to tell me that she was pregnant with our first child – no pressure there, then…

When the Ofsted inspector left, shaking my hand and walking out of the door saying, 'Good luck with the opening of the school,' I realised that I had actually done it.

That was in July; towards the end of the month and into August I began to meet prospective students and their parents or carers. I worked with the local authority to select the group of students who were most likely to benefit from the school, and in September the school opened with eight students and four members of staff. Now we have three schools and forty members of staff, and we're planning to open up three more schools in Devon. Judith and I were later joined by Rob Gasson as a director, who would support us to develop the project further. Rob had developed and was running one of the most successful chains of pupil-referral units in the UK.

From being principal of the first school, I went on to be executive principal of three schools and then chief executive officer of the organisation.

From trauma to transformation

As I continued to research ACEs, it struck me that, for far too long, my colleagues and I had been trained to ask young people and their families or carers the wrong question. Instead of asking them 'What's wrong with you?', we should have been asking 'What's happened to you?' I realised then what Life Chance Education's main goals should be:

- To provide positive interventions to remove the barriers to learning experienced by students with ACEs

- To reduce exclusions from mainstream education of students with ACEs

- To provide therapeutic education for students affected by ACEs

- To provide ACEs assessment and a therapeutic intervention service to local communities

- To contribute to community and social development through a trauma-informed approach

- To put an end to the intergenerational damage caused by ACEs

The concept

In Life Chance Education I have established a therapeutic education provider that specialises in working
with young people and families who have experienced
trauma in their lives.

My team and I are committed to transforming the life
chances of the young people and families who we work
alongside and in our wider communities. Life Chance
Education now runs a growing chain of independent
therapeutic day schools under the banner of School
for Inspiring Talents. It was the first school in the UK
to receive the Trauma and Mental-health-informed
Schools Award. All the students attend full time, and
I'm proud of the 'good' rating it has received from
Ofsted.

ACCREDITATION AS A TRAUMA AND
MENTAL-HEALTH-INFORMED SCHOOL

Trauma-informed Schools UK is an organisation committed to improving the health, wellbeing and ability
to learn of the most vulnerable schoolchildren in the
UK: those who have suffered trauma, abuse or neglect
or who have mental health difficulties or attachment
issues. Its co-directors are Dr Margot Sunderland and
Julie Harmieson. The Trauma-informed Schools Award
is presented jointly by the Centre for Child Mental
Health and Trauma-informed Schools UK. For more
information, visit www.traumainformedschools.co.uk

The schools are complemented by the ACE Clinic, a service that is staffed by a multi-disciplinary therapeutic team. They assess young people and families with a range of behaviour difficulties, emotional health difficulties and those affected by trauma. Life Chance Education also provides consultation, supervision, coaching and training to practitioners in a range of fields. The aim is to expand a trauma-informed approach across the social care, health, criminal justice and education systems, and into the wider community. The general public still have little understanding of ACEs and their impact, and it is part of my mission to remedy this. (Chapter 7 gives more detail about the outreach work of Life Chance Education.)

A supportive school

Life Chance Education schools cater for children aged five to sixteen who don't find it easy to fit into their mainstream schools. School for Inspiring Talents offers full-time placements for young people with an education, health and care plan who have been referred by local authorities. We offer ongoing support to them and their families by making recommendations in an individual multi-disciplinary assessment plan (MAP) that meet all their needs and can be put into practice in everyday life. I want every student to achieve their full potential, both academically and as a person. As the schools are day schools, they provide an alternative to residential education that encourages students to develop independence and social skills while living at home.

These amazing young people *can* succeed in following their dreams – but only with the appropriate support. That's what we're here for: to help them to develop the skills and talents that they will need to flourish in their lives, despite their challenges and difficulties (indeed, sometimes because of them).

School for Inspiring Talents schools are 'all-through' schools, which means they take children at primary and secondary level. Using a unique model, the schools address students' unmet needs through nurture, inspiration, motivation, and care. The holistic approach is what makes the most positive difference to the life chances of these young people.

My personal ambition for every child that comes through our doors is best summed up in our school motto: Being the best we can be.

Curriculum and practice

What's different about the School for Inspiring Talents is that it offers a therapeutic environment that combines best practice in education with current theories of learning, coaching, child development and neuroscience. Everyone learns differently, so we use a daily balance of structured play, guided activities and direct instruction to motivate learners and support each student to find the best way of learning for them. The School for Inspiring Talents provides a broad and balanced curriculum to help students to achieve outstanding educational progress for them. Because each child is an individual, the teaching is tailored to their individual strengths.

We get students hooked on the enjoyment of learning by balancing individual study with 'supported socialised working'. Enquiry-based approaches, where students learn together to solve problems and tackle dilemmas that have meaning for them, helps to engage them and relate to other people's perspectives. While the students are doing this, their brains are slowly and steadily rewiring themselves in a way that will enable them to function more fully in later life.

The aspirational environment and comprehensive services in our schools create a starting point for teaching art, mathematics, social studies, science and other subjects across the curriculum. This hands-on, real-world learning approach helps students achieve academically while developing stronger ties to their community. It also encourages them to appreciate the natural world and be active, contributing citizens.

LEGO THERAPY

The School for Inspiring Talents uses Lego therapy to help some students understand and develop social communication skills. Lego therapy relies on the students taking on different roles – an engineer, a supplier and a builder – and working together to build a model successfully. The engineer looks at the visual instructions, converts them into verbal information and describes the pieces for the supplier to find. The supplier's job is to direct the builder to place the bricks in the correct position. The supplier and the builder need to be able to take turns, wait and listen to the instructions. They need to be prepared to try again if they don't understand what they are being asked to do.

Many students will proclaim their expertise in Lego-building – 'I've built a whole pirate ship on my own before; I don't need anyone to help me!' – so we explain how building in Lego therapy sessions is different and that you need to use good communication skills to be successful.

The therapist (an adult) designs a structured play session to support students through negotiation and compromise as they decide who will take which role first. The adult models polite and friendly language, and praises students when they do so too. The students often learn from the behaviour that their peers model. For example, if one student is praised for asking nicely, the other is encouraged to try using polite language themselves.

The adult comments on and praises positive communication skills throughout the session, models desired behaviours, and makes suggestions, rephrasing and expanding what the students have said. These simple strategies provide positive social interaction for these children, most of whom struggle at times to play successfully with their peers. This supportive approach is not limited to the therapy sessions; it is part of all activities in a typical school day.

Because the schools are small, it is possible to provide highly personalised teaching to meet the needs of each student. When a new student joins the school, the student, their parents or carers and staff develop curriculum plans together to create a programme based on the student's strengths and needs. The following diagram shows the relationship between the four essential components of a student programme, and how they support high-quality learning and achievement.

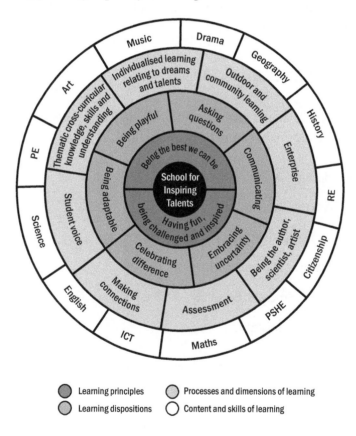

Figure 4.1 An integrated curriculum

Learning principles

Two principles create a thread that links all the learning experiences that are created for and by the students:

- Being the best we can be
- Having fun; being challenged and inspired

Together they form a solid basis for learning inside and outside the school.

Learning dispositions

Learning dispositions are the attitudes and skills that shape a person's approach to learning:

- Being playful
- Asking questions
- Communicating
- Embracing uncertainty
- Celebrating difference
- Being adaptable

Once developed and enhanced, these attitudes and skills bring a sense of predictability to the way a person engages in a new environment. Through understanding these dispositions and how important they are, a student (whatever their age) can begin to develop a way of being that helps them overcome challenges in a positive way (whatever the challenge).

Processes and dimensions of learning

The eight dimensions of learning provide balance across the academic curriculum, equipping students with techniques and experiences that allow their talents to emerge and be nurtured:

- Individualised learning relating to dreams and talents

- Outdoor and community learning

- Enterprise

- Being the author, scientist or artist

- Assessment

- Making connections

- Student voice

- Thematic cross-curricular knowledge, skills and understanding

Content and skills of learning

Through the thematic and place-based approach I described earlier, students learn subject-based knowledge and skills, just as in any other school. English, mathematics, science and information and communication technology (ICT) are the essential core subjects. Students can choose to take other subjects in which they have a special interest. They can choose from:

- Music

- Drama

- Geography

- History

- RE

- Citizenship

- PSHE

- PE

- Art

By providing positive purposeful experiences and removing barriers to learning, we aim to turn 'I can't' into 'I can'. I don't want any of our students ever to feel like the children I had met years ago at the school interview, who said that they weren't bright enough to pass exams or get a job.

A therapeutic approach

On top of helping students to get to grips with their school subjects, we also encourage them to develop self-awareness and a sense of responsibility. These are the qualities that will bring about positive behavioural change.

I believe that teaching should be tailored (in the broadest sense) to each child's individual strengths. I look for the abilities and talents inherent in them, and get them to see that they are capable of so much more than they thought possible. It's vitally important for students of all ages to develop an understanding of what it takes to 'be the best they can be' and of what makes them tick.

At the School for Inspiring Talents the therapeutic techniques and assessment tools include:

- Trauma-informed practice: is defined as an organisational structure and treatment framework that involves understanding, recognising and responding to the effects of all types of trauma

- Psychology: is the scientific study of the mind and behaviour

- Solution-focused brief therapy: is a form of specialised conversations that is directed towards developing and achieving the client's visions of solutions

- Occupational therapy: is the use of particular activities as an aid to recuperation from physical or mental illness

- Speech and language therapy: provides treatment, support and care for children and adults who have difficulties with communication

- Play-based therapy is a form of counselling or psychotherapy that uses play to communicate with and help people, especially children, to prevent or resolve psychosocial challenges

There's also an ACE screening tool, which I'll provide more information about in Chapter 7.

These therapeutic approaches and assessments help staff to address their students' specific developmental needs. This helps students to experience success, often for the first time. All these approaches are designed to improve students' physical, mental and emotional wellbeing, whatever their age. They also help students to develop emotionally and cognitively.

I'm determined, too, that students should have the opportunity to express themselves through creative activities and play. The creative process involved in self-expression allows students to resolve conflicts and problems, develop interpersonal skills, manage their own behaviour and reduce stress. Learning how to do these things builds their self-esteem and raises their self-awareness. They discover that it's safe for them to take risks when they're learning and that it's normal to make mistakes. Through this they find positive ways to communicate their emotional needs, become more emotionally resilient – and prove to themselves that they *can* learn and get enjoyment from learning.

Key points

- A trauma-informed school understands the close links between childhood adversity, trauma, brain development and learning, and designs its provision accordingly: therapy is educational, and education is therapeutic.

- Day-school provision enables students to develop independence and social skills while remaining at home.

- An engaging curriculum is one that takes an enquiry-based approach to traditional subjects and fosters a positive disposition towards learning.

- Using a range of therapeutic and diagnostic techniques allows us to tailor our approach to students' specific needs.

- Creative activities and play offer many benefits, including developing self-awareness and interpersonal skills, the ability to identify emotional needs, and growing confidence.

FIVE
School Days

Education is the most powerful weapon which you can use to change the world.
– Nelson Mandela

Educational theory is all well and good, but nothing compares with the experience of being in one of my schools. In this chapter, my colleagues explain why they work at Life Chance Education and the School for Inspiring Talents. They share how the approach works in practice, how much students have grown under their care, support and love – and how much they have grown too.

In the beginning...

Judith Johnson, Co-founder, Director and Chair of the Board

What worked well for us in those early days, when we were establishing the school and dreaming about how we wanted it to be and feel, was my knowledge of the education system from my professional careers in Ofsted inspections and as a Director for Education and Schools Services with two large local authorities. In addition to this was my experience from my background in service provision, school improvement, SEND, training and quality assurance, combined with Mark's passion for, and understanding of, the nature of the students we would be taking.

When the school opened, and Mark was in both principal and CEO mode, the challenge for us working together increased. We both had to work hard to ensure that our original vision did not get lost in the complexity of needing referrals to meet our cash-flow requirements but needing the students to be the right ones.

I could see from early monitoring that at the beginning there was little real 'curriculum-based learning' taking place, and I knew that the recommendations I wanted to make were beyond what we could realistically achieve then. We had some of the right people on the staff, but not necessarily the right educationalists in place – we had to grow our own staff, as no one comes ready-made for this environment.

Those early joint observations and monitoring sessions with Mark when he was principal were productive and enlightening for me: I watched the teacher and he watched the student – so we each saw different sides of the same coin. It was clear that a marriage of education and therapeutic provision was at the heart of what we were setting out to achieve.

My memory of those first couple of years is one of multiple staff roles and high staff turnover as we tried to get the right mix of skills. There were too many temporary contracts, too much damage to the fabric of the school and equipment, volatile classrooms, along with constant worry about funding and whether what we had set out to achieve was actually possible on the operating budget we had. The Ofsted 'Requires Improvement' judgement that we received after one year in operation was absolutely the right one.

We are both grateful that the support of our two main referring local authorities enabled us to survive those early years. What encouraged us was that although we knew we didn't yet have it exactly where it needed to be, the students kept coming. Their attendance was good compared with their previous settings – we must have been doing something right. We could see that these students were gradually finding their voice, adapting personally and emotionally, and realising the benefit of ground rules, space and safety to explore feelings and express themselves. Self-regulation of their behaviour increased, and parents and carers told us that they had noticed a positive difference at home.

Ofsted's subsequent 'Good' judgement recognised the journey we had made and enabled us to branch out with confidence. We were able to recruit a new executive principal, which freed Mark up to focus on the CEO role exclusively and develop the outreach and multi-disciplinary elements of the initial dream: to make an impact on the system.

Now, nearly five years on, all the school sites are calm, productive learning environments with a coherent, integrated curriculum that is matched to our students' needs. We now need to replace the wall displays only when the topic and work output requires it. The students have adopted the culture, and they even mentor new students in the School for Inspiring Talents way of doing things.

When I do my monthly quality assurance visits now, the first thing I notice is the evidence of learning around the classrooms and the purposeful atmosphere. I am always impressed by the staff when I sit in one of the daily staff debriefings – their collective passion, togetherness and openness are impressive. Learning support assistants and key workers are a significant aspect of our approach; our support staff are invaluable and are treated as fully part of the team. Yes, our students can still 'kick off' – after all, as our third and latest director, Rob Gasson, always says, 'It's in their job description – otherwise they would be in mainstream education.' But I am constantly moved by how much job satisfaction our staff gain when their work is so hard and potentially draining. They can be on the receiving end of occasional outbursts of physical and verbal abuse when relationships and emotions go awry, but this does not weaken their resolve, and relationships with students who lash out are always mended. I want to pay an enormous tribute to them.

Rising to the challenges

Pete Jenkins, Executive Principal

Working in a mainstream school setting for sixteen years, I have seen that the need to focus on standardised performance measures and deliver year-on-year improvements with decreasing funding provides a challenge that can lead to difficult decisions. Many schools have had to reduce staffing costs, and many schools have reduced the number of pastoral care assistants and classroom teaching assistants to balance the books.

Perhaps not surprisingly, one unintended consequence of these cuts has been an increase in challenging behaviour from students who would once have met regularly with pastoral assistants. These are students who have significant issues in their lives. Without a trusted adult to confide in, share experiences with and offload to, they are left lost in a school system that does not have the infrastructure to support them. Inevitably, schools have devised ways to negate their impact in the classroom.

'Ready to learn' is a school behaviour strategy that is, simply put, a clear zero tolerance policy that all students are trained in. Indiscretions lead to time out in inclusion rooms. For the 95% of students who can regulate their own behaviour, this works and their clear understanding of the sanction leads to improved behaviour in lessons. However, for the students who cannot regulate their own behaviour, repeated trips to the inclusion room are all too common. In schools that operate the system well, a student who often attends the inclusion room is flagged and their needs are investigated. But this does not happen in every school, and frequent trips to the inclusion room can be a route to permanent exclusion.

At the School for Inspiring Talents we recognise that, without the language skills needed to explain their feelings and emotions, a student's main method of communication can be behaviour – often challenging behaviour. Staff are highly trained in recognising such behaviour, de-escalating situations, and supporting students with therapeutic conversations. In fact, all the adults in the school receive training to enable them to take this approach.

A new journey

Stephanie Hart, Head of School (Primary)

Every child deserves a champion: someone who is unequivocally and unconditionally 'for' them. Yet the constraints of mainstream education have resulted in pressurised teachers who have become increasingly tasked to achieve unrealistic educational outcomes. This pressure to perform and achieve has, all too often, been to the detriment of a child's most basic human needs – to feel safe, accepted for who they are, loved and nurtured.

As a teacher and mother, I was witnessing the negative impact of this unbalanced ethos on the mental health of so many individuals, including my own son. Disenchantment had set in. That is, until I read about the School for Inspiring Talents: a school that was seemingly heralding in a new realm of possibility. And so, with some fear and a lot of trepidation, I started working at the school. My journey had begun.

I was met with explosive behaviour: verbal and physical outbursts from children who were suffering as a result of adverse childhood experiences. Yet the passion, love and care of the staff team and their advocacy for these young people set my heart alight. Change was most definitely afoot! The School for Inspiring Talents is undeniably a place of passion; it is palpable in everyone you meet, from the chief executive officer to the learning support assistants. Young and old alike, all the staff are there to make a difference.

The early days of my journey at the School for Inspiring Talents focused on behaviour and creating a haven for students. It was already a place that they wanted to come to; many of them felt more at ease in this school setting than they had ever felt before. Trusting relationships were growing where healthy attachments had previously been unknown. The team were interweaving therapy with learning, and staff were supporting students to manage their social and emotional needs. School systems were being established and honed, and Ofsted recommendations actioned; the trajectory looked promising. Parents saw that we were helping, and I was witnessing a change: our young people were beginning to flourish.

I had the privilege to be invited to set up our second school at Torquay and then to become, for a while, the Head of School. Starting with only a handful of students, Torquay has grown and is now confidently led by another member of the senior leadership team. Some of the most vulnerable children and young people in society are beginning to realise their full potential and are on the road to sitting GCSEs and other key qualifications. It is incredible to watch such transformation taking place.

Something new was happening for me too: in a move back into my comfort zone of organisation and systems, I became the newly created Head of Education Services. This role had an increasing number of strands, and it was one where I could enrol others to enable our students to be the best that they can be. Together we created a rounded curriculum that is exciting and offers memorable learning experiences. After all, what was the point of offering more of the same? The past recipe for learning had clearly been unsuccessful for these children. The new curriculum was officially recognised by Ofsted in 2018.

With ongoing support and encouragement from one of our credible and capable link directors, we established a new assessment system. The aim was to ensure that staff could measure students' progress carefully to spot and fill the learning gaps that had resulted from missed schooling and the devastating impact of trauma on their young lives. We continuously refine our assessment system, which is tailored to the specific needs of our learners.

Such highly personalised and therapeutic schooling has led to further growth and to recognition from external stakeholders. Referrals continue to flow in our direction, and I find myself once again in a new role – as head of the newly created primary school. Belonging to a community such as ours is never dull – that's for sure!

As in Torquay, we are starting small, but 'tall oaks from little acorns grow'. Transformation takes time, love and care. We are committed to meeting the previously unmet needs of our young people, and together we aim to develop their strength of mind, emotional wellbeing and resilience of character.

My affinity with the school's purpose moves and inspires me on a daily basis. I see continual positive transformation taking place – not just in the lives of our students, but in those of our staff team too. The care provided by the senior leadership team and the facilitation of routine coaching has most definitely changed me as a person. I believe that I have a better sense of who I am now, and if the School for Inspiring

Talents can do that for me then the future is truly bright for our young people.

We offer a new realm of possibility. Doing what education has always done will just get the same results: vulnerable children will fail. I am passionate about making a positive difference, and in working for the School for Inspiring Talents I know I can realise that dream.

Building relationships

Lewis Harben, Lead Teacher

Just like every other teacher, I grew up wanting to go into teaching so that I could make a difference and help to change children's lives for the better. From an early age I knew that this was the path I wanted to go down, and my GCSE and A-level choices were all selected with the aim of qualifying for teacher training. At Plymouth University I studied pedagogical theories and considered how I would apply these in my own classroom when I qualified. I can distinctly remember the excitement leading up to my first teaching practice in the classroom. However, from my first placement onwards I was often met with the same responses from teachers: 'Where do you think we are going to find the money for that?' When I'd ask about anything that wasn't on the national curriculum I'd be greeted with: 'Do you really think we have the time to do that?'

When I qualified I was lucky enough to be offered a job at a small village primary school where the staff truly believed in a holistic approach, valuing extra-curricular activities and additional opportunities for their pupils. The staff shared my values, but with the demands of standardised testing and tight budgets, it was impossible to provide the education that I had envisaged at university. My realisation soon developed into frustration, as my perception of teaching was challenged. I began to question whether it was possible to have the direct positive impact on children's lives that I had always imagined.

Then I saw a job advert for the School for Inspiring Talents. If anything, it seemed too perfect: it looked like a school that stopped at nothing to meet the needs of its pupils. This was exactly what I had gone into teaching for. I was convinced that this must be nothing more than an advertising campaign, that the reality would be just as inhibiting as my previous experiences. I could not have been more wrong. From the first time I looked around the school I could tell this place was different.

Everything about the school seemed authentic. The staff were genuinely happy, enjoying the freedom that they were given to do their jobs effectively; I remember sitting in my first debrief at the end of a school day and experiencing the support of the entire team, all actively striving to do the best for the students and for each other.

The strength of the relationships between adults and pupils was unlike anything I had ever witnessed. Staff really knew the children, and the care they had for them shone through. These children didn't just need us to teach them; they needed us to build much stronger relationships with them and to support them in every aspect of their lives.

I quickly developed a strong bond with a particularly energetic and inquisitive pupil who could argue with more passion than anyone I had ever met. Despite the connection that I had with him, the first few months were challenging, as it seemed that any answer I provided to his questions caused him to become frustrated and aggressive. At this stage he would swear at me, threaten me and physically attack me every single day, and it was often difficult to predict when this would happen.

One morning, after about four months of working at the School for Inspiring Talents, his behaviour was escalating. As I guided him into a reflection room he grabbed a fistful of my hair and dropped to the floor, pulling me down with him. Then he just lay there motionless, my hair still clenched in his closed fist. I placed my arm around him and assured him that no matter how many times he behaved like this, the staff at the School for Inspiring Talents would always be there to support him. I felt his grip loosen and he lay in my arms for several minutes, calmer than I'd ever seen him before. This was the turning point in my relationship with this pupil. Sure, his behaviour can still escalate at times, but from that moment onwards I've always known that he understands how much he is cared for. Breakthroughs like this make every challenging morning worthwhile.

This is just one example of the incredible experiences that happen every day at the School for Inspiring Talents. It is a school where no excuse is accepted – if an action is in the best interest of a pupil then it happens. In the School for Inspiring Talents I have truly found my opportunity to make a difference and help to change children's lives for the better.

Engaging hearts and minds

Jasmin James, Class Teacher

I applied to work at the School for Inspiring Talents in 2014, during the first term of its opening, and started on the first day back from the Christmas holidays. The only goals I ever had for my career were to work with children, be creative and help others. I hoped that this post would fulfil all three.

It was a different environment from any school I had seen before, which is partly what drew me to it in the first place. Located in a grand building surrounded by rolling hills and farm animals, it was quite a contrast to the environment that the students were used to. It felt right that these young people had a chance to experience the beauty of a rural setting that they otherwise would not pay much attention to. The school itself was set up on the top floor of the east wing and was much smaller than it is today, with a much lower staffing ratio. I still don't understand how we managed to keep the students safe and engaged in learning, but somehow we did.

We spent long days of exposing students to a different way of learning, trying to capture their interest and base everything on a practical approach. It appeared to engage them and remind them that learning can be fun. I quickly grew to love working with such a challenging group of youngsters, and I adapted to the challenging physical needs while learning to provide the high levels of emotional support that they so desperately craved.

The best thing I remember about those early days was being told by Mark that I could make the students feel 'loved' and like they were part of a family. This fell in line exactly with the ethos that I'd been raised with – all children need love and support to flourish – and this remains at the heart of my practice. Working in a mainstream setting, I was always aware of the need to maintain a professional distance from pupils, yet here I am encouraged to welcome students with a smile, share breakfast and a hug if they initiated it, and have a chat about the weekend. The school feels like a space where we as staff have been given the freedom to show we really care for our pupils, and I believe that this creates the trust and security that they so desperately need to grow as individuals.

During the five years that I have worked at the school, it has grown so much and I have grown along with it, but the core values have remained the same. They are to ensure that pupils are accepted and nurtured by staff who do not blame them for their behaviour but help them to understand why they do what they do, without feeling shame or guilt. I have seen a lot of staff come and go, because fundamentally it's difficult to remain so consistently calm and positive around such troubled children – but today I can honestly say that I am surrounded by an incredible team, who all give so much of their energy to making each student understand that they matter in the world and that we can be a catalyst for change in their lives.

I have progressed from being a learning support assistant to being a tutor, then a trainee teacher and then a teacher. For the past year, I have been teaching our 'nurture' class. I left for six months to travel with my husband and was welcomed back with open arms. I have been supported in living the best life that I can, and I think that it has been healthy for the children to see that there is a world of opportunities out there, and that exploring your dreams is possible.

Currently I have eight pupils in my class and, along with our learning support assistants, we have formed a tight-knit group. Humour and playfulness make up a large part of our interactions. Some of the most rewarding moments of my job have been seeing the students in my class turn from children who were 'school refusers', who were lacking in confidence and had never really had friends, into a group of 'best friends' who are excited about coming to school (even complaining profusely when we had a 'snow day') and engage in learning for most of the day. I'm delighted when a student tells me they are happy that they have made their 'first friend' and shares how excited they are that they will have people to invite to their birthday party.

We can offer something special to these students to show them just how special they are. I am brimming with pride when a student acknowledges that they have 'flipped their lid, and just need some time to get their thinking brain back', or when a student steps in to help regulate a peer, and uses the same language patterns as we do to calm them down. As staff, we want students to be aware of their actions and to become independent in regulating themselves. It's a long process, but it feels so great when you see the progress they make.

Offering regular learning breaks with sensory activities has enabled students to focus when it matters – with periods of relaxation or play in between. We have been given the freedom to design our own timetables based on what we think is best for our classes, and the results speak volumes. Students are generally happy in school, which means we can work on helping them to get to a point where they will be able to function and be happy when they leave school, too.

I can honestly say that parents' evening this year was one of the highlights of my life. Sitting and sharing such positive stories with parents and carers who previously dreaded meeting with schools made so many of the tricky days worth it. I feel so proud to be part of a team of people who are changing not only the attitudes of our students about education, but also those of their families.

This job brings out the most extreme emotions I have ever experienced. Our team laugh together and share the tough times together. I have cried over this job more than any other. The stress can be huge in an environment like this, but only because so many of us really care about our impact on the lives of these children – for many of them, we're the last chance before residential provision. I love my students, and I love my job; I hope that filters through all I do, because they deserve the best we can give them.

De-escalation

Tessa Cunningham, Lead Learning Support Assistant

To de-escalate a situation successfully you need to have the ability to organise your thinking and respond calmly to students who may be displaying aggression. Effective de-escalation techniques can help avoid a potential crisis. Things like awareness of personal space and body language, and listening skills, can help effectively de-escalate the disruptive behaviour of these students.

The following scenario with a twelve-year-old male student shows how de-escalation techniques deployed with care can defuse a potentially explosive situation. The student entered the classroom bouncing a football and the teacher asked him to put the ball back in the cupboard. This made the student react in an aggressive way, threatening the teacher with violence.

A colleague and I supported the student, who had been moved to a room to calm down. His mood was heightened and his intention was to get back into the classroom and – in his words – 'sort the bastard out'. We began speaking to him. I felt that he was too angry to talk about the incident, but I was aware that the incident needed to be discussed before he could move on. This is how the conversation went:

I said to him: 'Is it leather?'

He replied: 'Is what leather?'

Me: 'The ball.'

Him: 'I don't know.'

We discussed the merits of leather footballs over plastic ones, but my colleague and I then discovered that the student had a mobile phone on him, which was not allowed in school. We decided to go down the same route with the conversation, and discussed the make of the phone rather than the issue of him having it in class.

As the conversation developed, the student explained that he had wanted to hang on to the ball because he wanted one to hand for break time and there wasn't one in the playground. He went on to explain that the reason he had the phone was that his mother had promised to call him promptly after school and he was worried that if the phone was put away, he might miss the call. We said we understood his concerns but were worried he might lose the ball and lose or break the phone. We offered to let him have the football at break time and the phone before the end of the day, at which point he handed them over willingly.

If we had approached the situation – his having the ball and the phone – without understanding the reasons behind it, the outcome would have been different. We were able to help him calm down by using de-escalation; that is, concentrating first on discussing the ball and the phone, rather than on our problems with them.

I have used this technique many times. Its value is that it enables the student to take part in a non-confrontational conversation, so they can calm down at their own pace and come to their own conclusion about an incident. My role is to facilitate this and help students to develop their own internal mechanisms to deal with problems.

Dealing with special educational needs

Claire Upston, ACE Clinic Manager and Trauma-informed Practitioner

In my experience, being a special educational needs and disability co-ordinator (SENDco) in a mainstream school can be challenging. For me this was due in part to the barriers that I came up against when trying to meet the needs of some of the children on the SEND register who I was working with. The mainstream school that I worked at was located in an area of high deprivation, and with this came challenges for the children in the school. The most notable of these were experiences of domestic abuse, of the mental health difficulties of the parents, and of the neglect that can arise from these factors. In the later years of my time as SENDco in a mainstream school, I became particularly interested in the children whose special educational needs were described as social, emotional and mental health difficulties. There weren't necessarily resources or interventions readily available that could meet the needs of these children. As a result, their behaviour became more challenging and adults struggled to manage them. It was at this time that I first became aware of ACEs and the research available on them. Things began to make more sense to me.

Fast-forward a few years and I am in the privileged position of being head of multi-disciplinary services at the School for Inspiring Talents, where the language of trauma and ACEs is common among all the staff. On a daily basis I see the teaching and therapy staff implementing the most effective evidence-based approaches and making a real difference to the vulnerable and traumatised children and young people in the school. When I was working in a mainstream setting, I sensed that some children's special educational needs couldn't be attributed to cognitive or medical causes; rather, their needs resulted from the experiences that they had had, or continued to have. This sense has now become a shared conviction, based on evidence that developmental trauma has a real and proven impact on a child's ability to learn, have relationships, control their impulses and see their own true worth.

My role is ever-changing – something that delights me and drives me forward.

A focus on compassion

Amy Whiteley, Speech and Language Therapist

I started working at the School for Inspiring Talents as a speech and language therapist a couple of years ago. My posting required me to integrate this role into the therapeutic and educational environment to promote the development of children and young people who have experienced trauma in their lives. I realised that the task of influencing the mindset of some staff was going to be an important part of my role from the start:

the communication between adults needed to provide a positive model for these vulnerable students and facilitate their ability to interact successfully with their peers and the adults around them.

I then realised that these students struggled to play together effectively, let alone work together, as you need to do if you are to learn successfully. I regularly saw the students laughing at the misfortunes of others and showing limited compassion for their peers and the adults around them. Their lack of self-compassion was also evident; there were incidents where the students would show complete surprise when you did something for them.

One example of this happened when we were creating individual 'sensory boxes' for each student. On three or four separate occasions, a child came up to us to ask what we were doing. When we told them, they responded with something along the lines of 'I bet you haven't made one for me.' When we assured them that we had made one for everyone and showed them the box with their name on, the look of surprise on their face revealed that they had not thought that they would be worthy of this attention.

Reflecting on these incidents, I realised that we needed to focus on self-compassion and compassion for others before we could expect these students to be able to work effectively with one other. I developed a 'happiness programme' that aimed to target the three main aspects of self-compassion as defined by Dr Kristin Neff:[1]

- Self-kindness: the ability to accept that we are good at some things, and not so good at other things, and the ability to be kind to ourselves when we are unsuccessful or struggling

- Common humanity: the understanding that we are not alone, and that we are not the only person to have to go through negative experiences

- Mindfulness: the recognition of the here and now, being aware of negative emotions, and neither suppressing nor exaggerating the expression of these emotions

The initial six-week programme aimed to provide a safe environment to share personal details and anecdotes so that the students would be able to recognise similarities and differences in their experiences. The reasoning behind this was that some students are experiencing similar life challenges, yet they may not know that other students are experiencing them too. For example, a student who is living in foster care may not know that the boy sitting next to them is also in care. Obviously we are unable to share this information, but the students can be supported to do so and they feel

---

1 K. Neff, 'Definition of Self-compassion' (n.d.), https://self-compassion .org/the-three-elements-of-self-compassion-2

more able to manage if they know they are not the only ones in this situation.

The programme encourages discussions around different emotions and how we manage these emotions, emphasising that putting feelings into words can help us regulate the way that we express emotions and therefore expand our emotional vocabulary and understanding. This should help us to express our emotions more accurately with words, reducing the need to act out our negative emotions with negative behaviours.

These sessions were a riot to start with. Staff were inclined to sit back and watch the 'expert' (me) fail miserably. It was like a tag team – one in, one out – as the students struggled to sit in a circle, tolerate each other (and me) and work together. One class changed the name of the programme to 'hopefulness', as the students thought I was expecting too much from them.

But I persevered. Every week I would reflect on what worked and what did not; then I would adapt my session plan and try again. I explained to staff that we all needed to work together; I could not do this on my own and I valued their expertise and knowledge of individual students.

The next half term I renamed the sessions 'teamwork'. Research highlights the benefits of being explicit in telling our students what it is we are trying to achieve. We focused on active listening skills, and would start the session each week by going over what these skills are:

- Sitting appropriately and facing towards the speaker

- Staying quiet at the right time

- Listening for all of the words to make sure that we understand what is being said or asked

Our activities encouraged these skills and provided opportunities to practise. We also modelled, encouraged and supported discussions and reflective activities in each of the sessions. After a six-week programme, the before-and-after scores showed improvement in all areas. Subjective measures scored whether a student demonstrated a skill never, rarely, sometimes, most of the time (or all of the time with support) and independently. The scores were encouraging, but the anecdotal evidence even more so: we have observed our students engaging in conversations about their own traumatic experiences independently.

One child attempted to comfort another who had been taken into care that week by saying, 'I live with my grandparents because my mum prefers drugs to me.' Another child asked a boy in care why he missed his mum when she was mean to him, and he replied, 'Because she isn't mean to me now'; the first child then said that his mum did not feed him for days. A third child then joined in, saying, 'I live with my dad because my mum was mean too; all of us have mums who were mean to us.'

To me, these examples show these children processing what has happened to them and working through these experiences with peers who have experienced similar trauma, allowing them to realise that they are not alone.

In the final week of the most recent phase of the team-work programme, when they were each asked to choose one activity to do, we observed the whole class engaging in a discussion about all the activities that we had done over the last six weeks. Each student then chose an activity and they were then all able to agree the order in which we would do them. Staff sat back in amazement and then openly discussed this with the students to highlight how far we had come as a class in such a short space of time, laughing when we remembered the first disastrous sessions a few months earlier.

Taking the pain

Amy Brown, Learning Support Assistant

My day starts at 6.30am, when I stand looking in the mirror in my PJs, and then out of the window at the weather, to decide what would be appropriate to wear for my day ahead. This is when I find a top and my muddy jeans from the day before. As I put my jeans on, I look down at the mud and chuckle to myself as I think about how it got there. No, it wasn't from being kicked or pushed over; it was from the fantastic game of football we had during our sensory break.

I finish getting ready and leave to go to work. I car-share with another member of staff and we always have a good chat about the day before – sometimes we laugh so hard that our stomachs hurt, but on other days I get really emotional thinking about some of the children and the situations they face every day.

Once I arrive at work I go into the staff room, say good morning to everyone and then make my way up to the morning's briefing. Every morning I get asked the same question: do I want a coffee or tea? (The answer is always no!) I sit around with a team who are dedicated to their jobs, and I think how lucky I am to work in such an amazing place. I look up at the clock and it's getting closer to 9am, so I run down the corridor into the kitchen and sort out the children's breakfast. Then I grab my radio, coat and drink of water and walk to meet the children from their taxis.

Some days are brilliant and others aren't so great. My favourite part of all is helping these children who've been through tougher things then I'll ever go through. The image of the pain these children go through will forever be etched on my brain. Seeing them in trauma is painful to watch, but trauma doesn't define these children's behaviour or personality. Being kicked, punched, spat at and pulled to the floor is something that's become normal practice for me. It would shock most people, but I'm not most people. No one who works in this school is your 'normal' type of person.

No matter what happens, we always start the next session afresh. When the children leave at 3.30pm we have a debrief, talk about the day and tidy up for the next day. When I get home I take off my muddy jeans, my sweaty top and up-to-the-ankles-in-mud shoes. I look down at my legs and see the new bruises that have appeared and know it's been another good day in the life of the School for Inspiring Talents.

I wouldn't do my job if I cared about wealth, fame or glamour, but when I see these children succeed and thrive when they were once told they'd never amount to anything, I know my job is complete. Seeing them smile lights up my day.

Facing the challenge

Nathan Coombes, Learning Support Assistant

I don't think I would be able to describe any day at the School for Inspiring Talents as 'typical'. I might be able to write about how I'm doing at the end of some days. You might be interested to know that my shoes and trousers are often spattered in what I only hope is mud. That I need to wash the spit off the back of my neck on some days, and that I've had to retire *another* T-shirt. I could spend all day writing about the mysterious cuts and bruises that appear across my arms and legs. How I'm so tired on some days that I crash on the sofa the moment I get home. How I've come home feeling like a complete and utter failure. But I won't.

Instead, I'll write about how my trousers are covered in mud because I've been running around the grounds playing football and diving for Frisbees and rugby balls. That I made a child laugh so hard that they spat out their drink all over my face and down my neck. That I spilled coffee all over my T-shirt during morning briefing after remembering what happened. That sometimes to win at manhunt you need to crawl really far into that thorn bush. That kids have so much energy that it's hard to keep up during tag. That I can't, in fact, do the floss properly in front of the kids, however much I practise.

I wouldn't be honest if I didn't tell you that it's not all fun, games and dance-offs in the classroom during lunch. I've seen my fair share of tears. There have been times where I've been punched and kicked, spat at and threatened. I can't sugar-coat that – it's shit. I've been at my wits' end, sitting alone in the staff room trying to figure out why the hell I bothered getting out of bed that morning.

I teach children about mindfulness. About how to stop, take in deep breaths through our nose, fill our lungs, then our belly, and then... exhale. And then I'm back to joking and learning and laughing with them in PSHE about testicles and pubes and all the different synonyms for penis. Every child is with us because of unpleasant circumstances, and it's my duty and honour to help any of them in any way I can. Mud and spit, cuts and bruises – and be damned all the T-shirts I own.

Every day at Life Chance Education is going to be untypical. Luckily, we have a team of brilliant and dedicated individuals who are ready to face every day, over and over. For as long as it takes.

Key points

- People working with traumatised children need deep wells of compassion and resilience, and opportunities for reflection and recharging.

- It is often when they are at their most challenging that traumatised children are at their most needy.

- Children with ACEs are not used to having their needs met, so it may take dedication and effort to identify how they can best be helped.

- Observing a child with ACEs opening up and making progress is the most rewarding experience any teacher could hope for.

SIX

Unique Child, Unique Needs

There is no such thing as genius. Some children are
just less damaged than others.
    – R. Buckminster Fuller

What better way to illustrate how Life Chance
Education's approach works and the impact
it can have than to focus on the stories of three of
our students at the School for Inspiring Talents? I am
proud of these students for the changes that they have
achieved, and their stories confirm to me that I am now
fulfilling the promise I made to the chief constable all
those years ago.

Katie's story illustrates how a range of supportive
activities have contributed to her encouraging progress, while Sam's story looks in more depth at the
research underpinning our approach and how our

school shapes a programme to meet complex needs. Tom's story focuses on the therapeutic story that one of our lead learning support assistants has created to help him deal with his emotional difficulties. Although his specific experiences are not mentioned, this story demonstrates how stressful Tom can find situations that other children take for granted. I should add that the names of the children, and some of the details of their stories, have been changed to protect their identity.

Katie's story

This is the case study of a young girl I worked with closely when I was the principal at our first school. Katie was twelve years old and had missed a lot of schooling since moving up to secondary school. She was a withdrawn young woman, but she was perceived as being uncooperative and was being treated by CAMHS, who had given her a diagnosis of anorexia and depression. A number of other schools had been tried with Katie, but they had struggled to cope with her mental health needs. Katie recognised that the School for Inspiring Talents would be her last chance to gain some qualifications, and that she would also have to work with our in-school mental health practitioner.

ACEs

Katie had experienced six ACEs. Her dad had been sent to prison, and her mum had been in a number of violent relationships. She had suffered physical and emotional abuse and had been under the care of the local authority because of neglect. Katie had had to move house on numerous occasions, and her mum was being prescribed regular medication for mental health difficulties.

Attendance

When Katie first came to our school, she had a low attendance rate – 65.63% – so our family practitioner became involved in a supportive role, using a variety of specialist skills and resources. The family practitioner worked closely with Katie and visited the family home every week to provide a bridge between home and school. She also worked closely with Katie's mum, helping her to attend hospital appointments, supporting CAMHS appointments for Katie, and providing transport so Katie's mum could go to the school coffee mornings. Katie's mum would often contact the family practitioner for advice. Katie's attendance improved dramatically, going up to 89.41% within one term, with all the absences in that term being authorised.

Behaviour

When Katie first joined the School for Inspiring Talents she had low self-esteem. She would attend school wearing a onesie and spend a lot of time hiding under blankets and not doing much learning. Katie would also display extreme physical and verbal aggression towards staff and peers. This often resulted in restrictive physical interventions (RPIs) being used.

Logging the number of RPIs

Month	Number of RPIs	Direction of travel
September	8	N/A
October	8	←→ Stayed the same
December	5	←→ Decreased
January	1	↓ Decreased
March	0	↓ Decreased
July	0	←→ Stayed the same

Keyworker time

Katie had weekly meetings with her keyworker, where they reviewed and reflected on Katie's educational attainment and behaviour. They addressed any issues using a 'solution and strengths' approach. For example, the keyworker would start each meeting by asking Katie what she thought had gone well, and enabling her to think and talk about how she had achieved this. Building on a foundation of strengths allowed Katie to talk about what needed to be developed further. She was able to raise any worries or concerns, and discuss them freely, in this private meeting. They also discussed how they would agree what was working well and what needed to be tweaked or changed. Importantly, Katie's keyworker received regular therapeutic supervision to support her practice.

Therapeutic time

Katie had weekly sessions with the occupational therapist, the speech and language therapist and the trauma-informed practitioner employed by the school. This therapeutic provision is not normally available via more traditional routes in schools, and allows consistent multi-disciplinary work to be done, with regular communication and updates among all the practitioners. In the School for Inspiring Talents model, teachers are an integral part of the therapeutic team approach.

Over a period of a few months I saw a dramatic improvement in Katie's self-esteem and behaviour. She appeared to be more confident and began attending school wearing her uniform. There was a significant reduction in aggressive behaviour. Katie was able, at times, to communicate with staff when she felt unsettled. This was a direct result of her accessing our keyworker programme and therapeutic support while at school.

Katie began going to all the lessons on her timetable, and she was able to evaluate her attitude to learning, as well as her attainment, during every learning session. Yet she still seemed withdrawn on occasion, which led to some safeguarding concerns.

Summary report

Here is an extract from Katie's report after she had been at the school for six months.

> Katie is an able student who has made excellent progress this term academically and emotionally. She has made some good friendships with other students and is able to interact in a socially appropriate way with her peers throughout the school day. Katie is making continued progress in her communication skills with staff and students and can be a caring individual. She enjoys the therapeutic activities, particularly the drawing tasks, as she is very creative and finds that they settle her. Katie now has a personalised timetable which she is managing to follow, which has led to her achieving more learning and presenting as a much happier person in school.

Katie's voice

Katie said, 'I really enjoy coming to the School for Inspiring Talents. I wish we didn't have school holidays as I would rather come to school.'

Sam's story

This case study describes how Claire Upston, our ACE Clinic manager and trauma-informed practitioner, has worked with and supported one of our most vulnerable students.

Sam had a difficult start in life after being taken into care because of his parents' drug abuse. He had experienced eleven ACEs and two other circumstances that could also be classed as adverse experiences: he had only sporadic contact with both his parents before being taken into residential care. He is now in his fourth care placement. Because of his difficulties, he has also moved school three times and no local school feels it can take him. The local authority feels that his care placement is good and wants Sam to stay where he is, so they are looking for a local school that can understand the complex needs that arise from the trauma Sam has suffered and could work in partnership with the care home to support him.

Complex trauma is described by Bessel A. van der Kolk as 'the experience of multiple, chronic and prolonged, developmentally adverse traumatic events, most often of an interpersonal nature'.[1] Such a definition would certainly fit Sam's life to date.

---

1   B.A. van der Kolk, *Developmental Trauma Disorder: Towards a Rational Diagnosis for Children with Complex Trauma Histories* (2005), www .traumacenter.org/products/pdf_files/preprint_dev_trauma_disorder .pdf

ACE awareness in the school

An awareness of ACEs allows our school staff to view challenging behaviour in a new light. We draw up an ACEs timeline for all students to show which ACEs they have experienced and at what stage in their development. This allows us to judge whether they have missed the early rhythms and security of an attachment with the primary care giver – this was the case for Sam, who presented with attachment difficulties. We can then 'interact with these children [not] based on their age, but based on what they need, what they may have missed during "sensitive periods" of development'.[2] A high ratio of adults to students, along with the presence of a key worker from their 'class team', provides the safety cues that some of our students – like Sam – need to feel safe enough to risk engaging in learning.

PACE is an approach based on four key qualities (playfulness, acceptance, curiosity and empathy) that enable adults to support a child to develop self-awareness. The PACE approach, devised by Daniel Hughes,[3] gives us a framework for our relationship with troubled students

2   B.D. Perry, 'Applying Principles of Neurodevelopment to Clinical Work with Maltreated and Traumatized Children: The Neurosequential Model of Therapeutics', in N. Boyd Webb, ed., *Working with Traumatised Youth in Child Welfare* (New York: Guilford Press, 2006), 27–52, https://childtrauma.org/wp-content/uploads/2013/08/Perry-Bruce -neurosequentialmodel_06.pdf

3   D. Hughes, 'Dyadic Developmental Psychotherapy: Attachment-focused Treatment for Childhood Trauma' (2004), http://www .danielhughes.org/p.a.c.e..html

who need to know that no matter what, day in, day out, we are there and we care.

In Sam's case, each day is an opportunity for 'Team Sam' to chip away at the defences he has built around himself.[4] As Ludy-Dobson and Perry describe it, he is seeking to avoid close relationships, often by 'becoming aggressive and controlling as a way to protect [himself] from further hurt'.[5] We are aiming to reduce the dominance of toxic stress chemicals in Sam's brain and promote the release of opioids and oxytocin to move him from self-defence to social engagement.[6]

> Adverse environments resulting from neglect, abuse, and/or violence may expose children to toxic stress, which disrupts brain architecture and impairs the development of executive function.[7]
> – Center on the Developing
> Child, Harvard University

4   L. Bomber, *Inside I'm Hurting: Practical Strategies for Supporting Children with Attachment Difficulties in Schools* (Worth Publishing, 2007).

5   C.R. Ludy-Dobson, and B.D. Perry, 'The Role of Healthy Relational Interactions in Buffering the Impact of Childhood Trauma', in E. Gil, ed., *Working with Children to Heal Interpersonal Trauma: The Power of Play* (New York: Guilford Press, 2010), https://childtrauma.org/wp-content/uploads/2014/12/The_Role_of_Healthy_Relational_Interactions_Perry.pdf

6   J. Panksepp, *Affective Neuroscience: The Foundations of Human and Animal Emotions* (New York: Oxford University Press, 1998).

7   National Scientific Council on the Developing Child, *Excessive Stress Disrupts the Architecture of the Developing Brain: Working Paper 3*, Updated Edition, (Center on the Developing Child, Harvard University, 2005/2014), https://developingchild.harvard.edu/science/key-concepts/executive-function

As described in Chapter 3, developmental trauma has a big impact on a person's executive functions. Knowing about a student's ACEs and when they occurred allows us to consider how much the development of these crucial functions may have been affected. This then allows us to pitch the academic curriculum and our expectations of their progress at the correct level.

Emotional development

Being in care can be seen as an additional ACE, because it is likely to limit the young person's access to the consistent emotional availability that they need for their neurological development. Although Sam has good relationships with the team of carers in the home, this cannot replicate the attachment relationship that he could build with one key care giver – particularly as physical contact between Sam and his carers is restricted in line with the home rules. Through activities that form part of our trauma-informed practice, Sam is developing an attachment relationship with his teacher, who is also his keyworker. Sam craves close physical contact with his teacher but does not know how to initiate it. He finds this harder because his teacher is male.

Sam is also physically active. His teacher has introduced regular, timetabled activities with Sam to help build a relationship. These are based in part on activities from Margot Sunderland's *Best Relationship with your Child* DVD.[8] These activities also give Sam the chance to interact with others in a fun and playful way through the laughter and eye contact that arise from a game of pom-pom, blow football or balloon balance.

To chart our students' emotional development, we use *The Stages of Emotional Development* resource provided through the Trauma and Mental-health-informed Schools programme.[9] Sam is currently at stage two: he is able to label a few main emotions within a limited emotional vocabulary.

Sam regularly defaults to 'fight or flight' when he feels a strong emotion. We are working with him to help him understand why he uses these responses. In a recent session, we showed him a Play-Doh model of the structure of the brain and introduced him to the term 'flipping your lid'. Encouragingly, Sam has been using 'flight' – that is, running away from the school building – less often as the strength of his attachment relationship with his teacher has grown. His teacher has become skilful at using curiosity – the 'C' of PACE – to wonder aloud about the feelings and sensations that Sam may be experiencing at any given time and whether they are the reason for him needing to run.

The PACE approach belongs to the 'Relate' part of the Protect/Relate/Regulate/Reflect model that we have

---

8   M. Sunderland, M (2015), *Best Relationship with Your Child* (2015) [DVD].
9   A resource sheet provided by www.traumainformedschools.co.uk

incorporated into the school's new relationship policy. A key part of our Relate work with Sam is to encourage him to trust a range of adults. Given Sam's experience of threatening and unpredictable environments as a young child, it's no surprise that he mistrusts adults who he doesn't know. To begin with, whenever I entered the classroom he would immediately ask me, with great hostility, 'What do you want?' This is a clear example of blocked trust, described by Baylin as 'the child's bias towards automatically treating ambiguity in other people's communication as a threat'.[10] I now avoid neutral facial expressions and am specific about my reason for entering the classroom because, as Bomber notes, 'neutral faces are anxiety-provoking for many children and adolescents who have experienced significant relational traumas and losses'.[11]

We support staff to be emotionally available and to avoid developing 'blocked care' – a state where a carer may be unable to feel empathy due to prolonged stress levels in the face of the repeated rejections from students in response to attempts to develop an attachment relationship with them.[12] We also train staff to avoid telling students 'You need to calm down' or 'When

10　J. Baylin, *Parental Compassion and Attachment Focused Treatment: Why it's Crucial to Help Parents Resolve their Ambivalence Towards the Mistrusting Child* (DDP Network, 2015), https://ddpnetwork.org/backend/wp-content/uploads/2015/08/Jon-Baylin-Parental-Compassion-and-Attachment-Focused-Treatment.-30-July-2015.pdf

11　L. Bomber and D. Hughes, Settling Troubled Pupils to Learn: Why Relationships Matter in School (Worth, 2013).

12　D. Hughes and J. Baylin, *Brain-based Parenting: The Neuroscience of Caregiving for Healthy Attachment* (New York: WW Norton, 2012).

you've calmed down... ' and to work through the stages of physiological regulation, co-regulation and self-regulation with the students (see the example described in 'De-escalation' in Chapter 5). In this way, students benefit from the 'social and emotional support of a safe connection with a caring adult.

The next phase is the 'Regulate' aspect of the model. At times when their emotions are heightened, students are offered relational breakout periods with their key-worker in which to build their relationship and access a calm and private space to help them regulate their emotions. We have personalised the Zones of Emotional Regulation programme to reflect where each student is on The Stages of Emotional Development chart.[13]

---

13   L. Kuypers, *The Zones of Regulation: A Concept to Foster Self-regulation and Emotional Control* (San José: Think Social, 2011).

Stages of emotional development

Stage One	Stage Two	Stage Three	Stage Four
Emotion experienced as sensation (feelings are 'behaved' rather than thought about).	Primary emotions at times labelled accurately, while other emotions are labelled inaccurately within the limited vocabulary the child knows.	Feelings regularly labelled accurately. More in-depth emotional states can be thought about.	Theory of mind skills/capacity for mentalisation.
Actions for staff:	**Actions for staff:**	**Actions for staff:**	**Actions for staff:**
Help the child move from sensation to awareness. Model putting feelings into words. Use 'mental state' talk. Don't expect them to come up with words for feelings.	Help the child to keep in mind the defence and the feeling underneath the defence. Keep labelling feelings.	Use a richer vocabulary and images for feelings when talking to the child.	Praise their capacity for reflection and join the child in their reflective process.

For students who still experience their emotions as sensations, we use 'visual zones charts' (as explained in the table) that feature bodily sensations rather than emotion words. We are lucky to have beautiful grounds around our schools, so we make full use of the outdoors and green spaces to help our students regulate their emotions.

The 'Reflect' aspect of the model involves an attuned keyworker helping students to identify the triggers, emotions and sensations that affect their interactions and responses, day to day and their life so far. Sam, like many of our students, has led a complicated life, full of confusing and disturbing events. For him to avoid a negative view of himself, he must arrive at an understanding of what has happened and why. Using sand tray work, artwork and visual images like the Emotion Cards,[14] we are exploring the narrative that Sam has developed for himself and helping him to create a coherent story by carefully sharing the facts, creating timelines, and listening in an empathic and attuned way.

Overcoming fear

Sheridan and McLaughlin make a distinction between the impacts of threat and deprivation on a child's development.[15] Sam experienced threat and deprivation in his early life, as he was repeatedly exposed to domestic violence, frequently visited A&E with his

---

14 M. Sunderland and N. Armstrong, *The Emotion Cards* (London: Routledge, 2018).

15 K.A. McLaughlin, M.A. Sheridan, and H.K. Lambert, HK (2014), 'Childhood Adversity and Neural Development: Deprivation and Threat as Distinct Dimensions of Early Experience', *Neuroscience Biobehavioral Reviews*, 47 (2014), 578–91, https://www.ncbi.nlm.nih.gov/pubmed/25454359

own injuries, and experienced severe emotional and physical neglect because of his mother's poor mental health and substance misuse. He also moved between carers fourteen times before he was placed in residential care. We use Panksepp's model of six emotional systems to consider the different impacts that these two aspects of trauma produce, and the imbalance of emotional states that results.[16]

When he first joined us, Sam was described as 'terrified', with 'no foundation or expectation that the care he receives from the adults around him will be safe or will meet his needs'. In Panksepp's terms, Sam had an over-active fear system and an under-active self-care system. Sam has made progress since being with us, but there is still work to do to correct this imbalance. 'Team Sam' works each day to try to show Sam that he is worthy of care and that they are with him and for him, no matter what. They are consistent and predictable, and show empathy and acceptance, helping to reduce Sam's ingrained feelings of fear by creating an atmosphere of safety. Perry says: 'This is done most easily and effectively in the context of a predictable, respectful relationship. From this nurturing "home base", maltreated children can begin to create a sense of competence and mastery.'[17]

---

16 Panksepp, *Affective Neuroscience*.
17 B.D. Perry, 'Applying Principles of Neurodevelopment to Clinical Work with Maltreated and Traumatized Children: The Neurosequential Model of Therapeutics', in N. Boyd Webb, ed., *Working with Traumatised Youth in Child Welfare* (New York: Guilford Press, 2006), 27–52, https://childtrauma.org/wp-content/uploads/2013/08/Perry-Bruce-neurosequentialmodel_06.pdf

Tom's story

Lucy Begam, Lead Learning Support Assistant, has worked alongside our educational psychologist to help support Tom, a student with behaviours of disorganised attachment. She created a therapeutic story based on one of his key interests: cars and motor racing. The story features events that parallel what has happened in Tom's own life: events that caused trauma and led to emotions and behaviours that Tom struggles to control.

The aim of the therapeutic story is to help a student recognise areas of the story that are similar to their own life. Some children can recognise these on their own; others need support. This is when the PACE approach supports the story by encouraging students to listen with skill and ask exploratory questions. We use the PACE model to communicate with students in a playful way that keeps them at ease, helping them to accept why they show certain behaviours and that these behaviours do not define them as a person. We use curious speech to help them with self-reflection, allowing them to think about their own actions and emotions. Lastly, we use empathy to let the student know that we care deeply about them and their choices.

Asking curious questions in a playful tone helps the student to identify some kind of link between the story and their life, emotions and actions. In Tom's case, the story demonstrated to him that he could widen his circle of trustworthy adults. It helped him recognise possible triggers for extreme emotions and behaviours so that he could self-regulate when his feelings started to run high.

LENNY THE LAMBORGHINI

This is a story about Lenny, a dark blue Lamborghini. Lenny lived in a car showroom, though he wasn't for sale. Lenny had two people to keep him clean, well fuelled, waxed and polished. Lenny hadn't always had people who looked after him so well. When Lenny was still at the factory he wasn't well looked after at all and he didn't feel safe. The people at the garage could see that Lenny was feeling sad because water leaked from his engine and his lights were dim. Sometimes he would rev his engine so much he would overheat. Lenny couldn't always cool himself down so sometimes he had to drive off outside. The garage people moved him to the showroom where they could take care of him.

Lenny liked it at the car showroom. He cared about other people so he made sure he had comfy seats and his computer often said kind things to his passengers, like 'You're a really good driver.' He thought it was important to make other people feel good about themselves. Lenny liked to look after the other cars in the showroom, so when the other cars' computers said unkind things to each other Lenny would bump into them to stop them. But sometimes he would overheat.

This also happened when Lenny had to go to the race track and race with other cars. There were lots of other cars there, and there were also people who changed their tyres and made sure their brakes were working, so that Lenny and the other cars were safe. There was one particular mechanic who Lenny felt safe with and he always wanted him to change his tyres. When this mechanic wasn't free to take care of him, sometimes Lenny didn't want to race. Sometimes there were so many cars and mechanics that it all became too much for him. His computer would lose control and make him say unkind things and bump into other cars and mechanics. Sometimes he would over-heat so much that his engine would start steaming. The mechanic who cared for Lenny could see when it was all getting too much for him and would take him to the garage to help him cool down and to keep the others safe.

No one at the showroom or the race track thought Lenny was bad. They knew that sometimes the race track was too much for him and because they cared, they wanted to keep him safe. They could see that it was hard for Lenny to race, but they knew that if he did he could be the next super racer. After all, he was a Lamborghini!

One day a new car arrived at the race track and Lenny saw a mechanic put different tyres on it. He couldn't understand why this car had been given new tyres but he hadn't. So he asked the mechanic, who told him it was because the other car found their old tyres uncomfort-able. The mechanic also tried to explain that Lenny had never said anything about his own tyres being uncom-fortable. But Lenny was still annoyed by this, which made his computer lose control and he began to swear. He thought that his tyres were uncomfortable too, and began to shout that everyone's tyres were uncomfortable. He couldn't believe how unfair the mechanics were being.

Lenny felt his engine overheating and looked for his favourite mechanic, but he was nowhere to be seen. He was changing another car's tyres at a different part of the race track. Lenny felt worried, annoyed and unsafe.

'Who will look after me?', he thought. Lenny overheated and the other mechanics had to take him away.

Later that day, back at the showroom, Lenny was feeling tired and sad. He hated not being able to have his favourite mechanic when he needed him. He worried that he didn't care about him any more. Just before he went to sleep Lenny heard the showroom doors open and a really loud engine noise. He looked up and saw an army tank! The tank had a big and wise computer and could see that Lenny was feeling worried, so he said, 'I can see you're feeling annoyed, because you look like you've overheated. What happened?'

Lenny said, 'I'm worried that my favourite mechanic at the race track has forgotten about me.'

The tank said, 'I used to have a soldier who looked after me at the camp and it made me feel safe and special. One day she got sent off to another camp because she was so good at helping tanks, but I didn't know and I thought she didn't care any more. But one day I saw a letter to the captain asking how I was and telling him to take good care of me. Then I knew that even though she wasn't there she cared about me. I bet your mechanic feels the same.' Then the tank drove off.

The next day at the race track, Lenny was asked to race. Usually his favourite mechanic would check his brakes, but again he wasn't around to help. Lenny thought about what the tank had said and felt he would be brave and let himself trust another mechanic – just a bit, for today. He thought that he would trust that his favourite mechanic still cared for him, and he knew he was being brave to do so. Lenny raced, and he was amazing!

Lenny had fun with the other cars and realised that maybe they could be his friends. But he still thought about his favourite mechanic, and on his way back to the garage he saw him! Lenny was happy, but a bit anxious about whether he did still care – especially because Lenny had trusted that he did. The mechanic said to Lenny, 'I've heard from the other mechanics how well you did today, which made me feel very proud of you! Sorry I wasn't there to watch you, but I've been thinking about how you were doing all day and it's so nice to see you. But you also look a bit worried – what's up?'

Lenny said he thought perhaps the mechanic didn't care about him any more. The mechanic told Lenny that just because he wasn't always there didn't mean he wasn't thinking about him, and that he would always care.

Lenny felt warm inside, as if he'd had a nice oil change and his battery was recharged. He felt proud of himself for having a good day at the race track, and now he knew he could cope even if his favourite mechanic wasn't always there to help, because he knew the mechanic thought about him. He drove back to the showroom and his lights shone brightly all the way. The two people who looked after him there noticed his bright lights and said, 'You must have had a lovely day, look how brightly you're shining!'

Two weeks later, Lenny began to feel confident that although his favourite mechanic was busy sometimes, he would always care about him and be thinking about him. This helped Lenny to concentrate on racing and spend less time worrying. He knew that his favourite mechanic sent messages to the people at the showroom, telling them how well Lenny was doing. The people at the showroom were proud to call Lenny their car, and this made him happy. Lenny knew that even if he overheated sometimes, people would still care for him.

The three stories in this chapter have shown how the ACE model has given our staff evidence-based frameworks in which to place the work they have been doing. It has given us the knowledge and confidence to try something different from the approaches that have already failed traumatised and vulnerable children like Katie, Sam and Tom. The journey – for them, for all our students, and for ourselves – has only just begun...

Key points

- Children with ACEs often try to avoid close relationships, for fear of experiencing further hurt and rejection.

- It is vitally important for traumatised children to be able to develop a strong attachment relationship with an available adult.

- Teaching children to identify their emotions and communicate them to others is essential for their wellbeing and progress.

- A child will not be able to cope with a traditional school syllabus unless they have first learned to organise themselves to use their working memory and focus their attention at will.

- PACE – playfulness, acceptance, curiosity and empathy – underlies all our interactions with the children.

SEVEN

Reaching Out With CARE

Children are not a distraction from more important
work. They are the most important work.
– John Trainer MD

The CARE Model

Whenever young people and families are referred to
us, our first step is to apply the CARE model, as illus-
trated below.

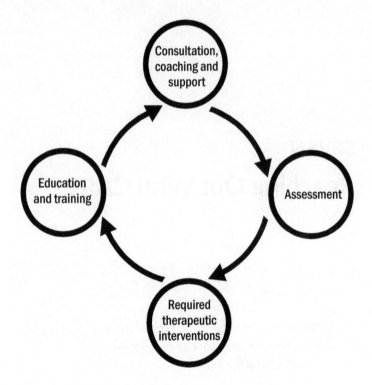

Figure 7.1 The CARE model

This model recognises that we're not dealing with a child in isolation, and that the impacts of ACEs ripple outwards to affect those in the family and in professional settings – and in the community. That means we aim to support not only the students in our schools, but their peers in other schools and the parents, carers and professionals around them.

We offer this support in our own schools, at other schools and relevant organisations, and by working with families, groups and individuals.

Consultation, coaching and support

- Providing consultations to assess trauma-informed practice in your school or organisation

- Providing coaching to support trauma-informed practice in your school or organisation

- Giving advice to support trauma-informed practice in your school or organisation

Assessment

- Assessing students at our schools after consultation with referring schools and agencies

- Assessing young people and families at the ACE Clinic after consultation with referring schools and agencies

- Assessing young people and families in the referring services' environment

Required therapeutic interventions

- Providing therapeutic interventions for students at our schools

- Providing therapeutic interventions for young people and families at the ACE Clinic

- Developing therapeutic interventions and care plans for referring services: education, health, social care, foster carers and the criminal justice system

Education and training

- Educating students at our schools

- Training multi-professional audiences on ACEs and trauma-informed practice

- Educating and training young people and families to help prevent ACEs

Looking back, I wish that people had known about ACEs when I was going through my struggles. Today, I'm determined to spread knowledge and understanding far and wide.

Let's look in detail at how Life Chance Education reaches out to communities to share the benefits of the CARE model.

The ACE Clinic

Claire Upston, ACE Clinic manager, is keen for as many children as possible to benefit from our approach. Here, she describes how we have extended our reach through the ACE Clinic:

> The nature of the work we do means that our schools have to stay small to maintain the relationships between staff and students, and to ensure that we can continue to provide the safety cues that these children and young

people need. That means there is a limit to the number of students who can enrol in our schools. So it was time to look outwards to the wider community and offer support to the mainstream schools around us.

This is how the ACE Clinic was born. Today, the clinic offers consultations, training and coaching to mainstream schools to improve their ability to meet the needs of students whose social, emotional and mental health difficulties stem from traumatic events. The clinic's multi-disciplinary team includes a trauma-informed practitioner, a speech and language therapist, an occupational therapist, an educational psychologist, a family practitioner, a mental health practitioner and a consultant clinical psychologist. This team can assess children and young people who are referred to us and then work closely with their school and their parents or carers to adjust the support they receive in school and at home. The more children and young people we can work with, the more we can upskill staff, spread the word about the real source of these students' difficulties, and change the way that education works for students who have had a disrupted and painful start in life.

Consultation, coaching and support

We provide consultation, coaching and support to other professionals to improve trauma-informed practice where they work. We travel to other schools, and we meet with social workers, foster carers, people working in the criminal justice system and youth-offending teams. We also work with adoption agencies.

For example, we may arrange a consultation clinic at a practitioner's premises so that staff teams can come and talk to us about individual young people and the sorts of interventions that would meet their needs. We share advice and signpost people in the right direction. We may also refer them to other organisations for support with specialist issues. For example, a charity would be able to provide detailed expertise on domestic violence.

Sharing expertise

On average, members of the Life Chance Education team spend 60% of their time working in the School for Inspiring Talents and 40% of their time doing outreach work and training. This means the consultation, coaching and training are provided by people who are continuing to work 'at the coalface', dealing with some of the most difficult, damaged and vulnerable members of our communities.

We coach other professionals on how to enhance trauma-informed practice in their organisation. For example, we've coached people on:

- How to set up sensory rooms for young people, using beanbags, rocking chairs and weighted blankets to create a safe space where people can feel secure enough to open up about their experiences

- How to talk to students about their trauma in a way that helps them to overcome their problems and make progress

We make the most of all the experts in our team, providing advice from occupational therapists, speech and language therapists, mental health workers, and others. A key team member is our family practitioner, who not only advises other professionals but also works with families – those of the children in our schools, and those of children referred to us who attend other schools.

Assessment

After a consultation with the referring agency, we may refer a young person and their family to the ACE Clinic. Our assessment staff spend time assessing the students in our schools. They use an assessment tool that tracks when the ACEs happened in young people's lives against the normal developmental milestones.

All the assessments, inside and outside our schools, are done by a multi-disciplinary team so that we can get a picture of all the support the young person needs – say, speech and language therapy and mental health support. We give all young people a MAP – a multi-disciplinary assessment plan – to follow with their families and with their teachers, social workers and other professionals. We give these important adults in young people's lives coaching and ongoing supervision to help them use the MAP.

Required therapeutic intervention

Once we have done a full assessment, we identify the therapeutic interventions that the young person needs and the therapists who will provide them. Our own therapists give some of this support, such as speech and language therapy, and occupational therapy. We also work with therapists outside the school if doing so will benefit a particular child. These colleagues have specialist skills, for example in drama therapy and art therapy. This way of working makes sure that we are always led by the young person's needs.

Education and training

In this context, I'm talking about educating teachers and other professionals – those who have many children with ACEs on their school register or as part of their caseload.

We provide training and guidance from a range of professionals. We visit schools to give presentations on ACEs and trauma-informed practice, and we follow that up with more detailed work.

We also run courses to help professionals learn about trauma-informed practice. The Trauma-informed Practice course is an introduction to meeting the needs of students whose difficulties were caused by developmental trauma or ACEs. The course focuses on:

- How trauma affects brain development

- The link between trauma and difficulties with executive functions, such as problem solving and maintaining attention

- How to be an emotionally available adult

- How to be in a relationship with a traumatised child

- How to provide safety cues in school

- How to have an empathic conversation

- The PACE approach

- Evidence-based interventions

The Trauma-informed SENDco course explores how these professionals can best meet the needs of students whose difficulties were caused by developmental trauma or ACEs. It focuses on:

- How to have the conversations needed to discover whether a student has experienced ACEs

- Why the timing of different ACEs is important

- The link between trauma and difficulties with executive functions

- How to write an individual provision plan for a traumatised child
- Interventions and strategies for teaching and support staff to use

We also train professionals and parents about neuroscience and how children's brains develop. This gives professionals who are responsible for children more understanding of the changes that children's brains go through and how this is likely to affect their thinking and behaviour.

The Neuroscience and Child Brain Development course looks at how trauma and ACEs affect a child or young person's brain development. It covers:

- Typical brain development at different ages and stages
- The changes that take place in a teenager's brain
- How ACEs affect brain development
- What can be done to reverse or repair the impact

We are tailoring more and more of our training to specific organisations. We meet with the organisation or group to find out about their particular circumstances, so we can shape training to cover exactly what they need.

Key points

- The more widespread the knowledge about ACES, the more we can all help traumatised children and young people to overcome their problems and make progress in their education, relationships and lives.

- Working with traumatised children can be tough, and professionals need adequate supervision and support if they are to cope with the demands placed on them.

- Trauma-informed education requires not only well-trained teaching staff, but also a specially tailored school environment.

- An understanding of neuroscience and brain development is essential for making sense of the emotions and behaviour of children and young people affected by ACEs.

Conclusion

If someone had told me all those years ago that I'd be the chief executive officer of a group of trauma-informed schools, I wouldn't have believed them. And if I had dared to believe it for a second, the thought would have been so overwhelming that I'd have been terrified.

But all those years have taught me a lot. If I could reach out to the boy who I once was, I would tell him that the things that happened to him were not his fault, that he was not a bad boy. That he deserved to be loved and cared for, to be respected and to feel valued – that he mattered. And I would tell him that time is a healer, and that he will be OK.

My mission throughout my career has been to bridge the gap between the world I grew up in and the professional services, many of which struggle to understand the barriers that stand in the way of traumatised children reaching their potential. I want students and practitioners alike to see that anything is possible. I want these amazing young people to succeed in reaching for their dreams, to develop the skills and talents that they will need to flourish in their lives.

Yet I've heard time and again that current education provision is not able to meet the needs of some of our most vulnerable young people, and more and more of them are slipping through the net: my experiences continue to highlight rising numbers of students who are excluded because they find it difficult to fit into existing education provision.

Young people arrive at school with varying levels of ACEs. They need staff and other professionals who support them to be trauma-informed, responsive and compassionate. They need these people to help them to overcome the trauma that is threatening their social and emotional health and their academic success, just as Fred helped me. Schools need to create a culture that teaches resilience. Every member of staff in the school can help children build resilience so that they are able to manage the impact of their ACEs, attend school and improve their life chances.

A community response

If ACEs continue to be poorly understood in some educational and mental health settings, the picture is even more confused in wider society. What is the difference between trauma and painful life experiences that don't lead to trauma? Trauma is not an event itself, but an emotional response to an overwhelmingly painful and stressful event that took place when there was no one to help. This is why we need to make sure that students have as many trauma-informed people around them as possible.

We can all play our part in ending child trauma. Every interaction is an intervention: we are all capable of providing therapeutic moments in our everyday interactions with children and young people. ACEs and their potential cost to individuals and society need to be widely understood in communities and in every corner of government and administration.

Dr Burke Harris MD, founder and former chief executive officer of the Centre for Youth Wellness, says that the cure for toxic stress can't be delivered by doctors and the healthcare system alone; it requires a community-level response: 'This understanding needs to be infusing every aspect of our community and culture.'[1] She believes that no one programme will fix these problems, and that we will see significant progress only when we are implementing solutions in faith communities, after-school programmes, residential settings and the care that adults provide for young people, whether it is in the family or in a professional context.

---

1   N. Burke Harris, TED Talk, 'How Childhood Trauma Affects Health Across a Lifetime', 2014, https://ed.ted.com/featured/eczPoVp6

It's good to talk

At a recent conference run by ACEs expert Dr Margot Sunderland, she talked about the 'can of worms' myth: the myth that talking about the traumatic events in their lives only makes children start thinking about them again. We can explode that myth for a start: in reality these children will already be thinking about their traumatic events a lot of the time – as I can confirm from my own experience. With our help, they can think about these events in a supported way; they should not be left to dwell on or interpret events that are too traumatic for them to make sense of on their own.

People start to heal the moment they feel heard. Hence, my explosive new mantra:

Trauma

Needs

Talking about

Exploding the myth of talking about trauma

Children want us to know; they want to be allowed to talk and they want us to ask questions. A research study conducted by Dr Stuart Hauser with seventy teenagers who had been placed on psychiatric wards showed that talking about their experiences enabled the teenagers to find 'agency' – in other words, discovering that 'one can intervene effectively in one's own life'. One of them said, 'We reflect on our experiences and our reflections lead us to new understandings and new possibilities.'[2] Without this understanding, children can blame themselves for what has happened, just as I did after suffering abuse as a child.

No matter what your role in caring for vulnerable children, I encourage you to find out more about how you can begin the healing process with them. Explore what's on offer on the Life Chance Education website at www.LCEducation.org.uk, or contact me by emailing mark.escott@LCEducation.org.uk. No mission is more important than to reach out to our young people and restore their potential.

I'll leave you with a quote that says it all:

> A hundred years from now it will not matter what my bank account was, the sort of house I lived in, or the kind of car I drove… but the world may be different because I was important in the life of a [child].[3]
> – Forest E. Witcraft, teacher and scholar

---

2   S. Hauser, J. Allen, and E. Golden, *Out of the Woods* (New York: Harvard University Press, 2008).

3   F. E. Witcraft, 'Within my Power' *Scouting Magazine* (1950), 2.

Afterword

I am in awe of Mark, and of how he became the person he is today from the troubled boy that he once was. I love to watch him with his own children and to see what a wonderful father he is; on top of that, he is so passionate about other people's children and how he can improve their lives.

I don't think people really have any idea how their children will turn out when they are first born. He was the most beautiful baby, and in the early years, when it was pretty much just him and me, I wanted to do all I could to protect him. He was such a gentle, loving and giving child. I didn't have any particular thoughts about his future. I'm a hairdresser, and I suppose if I'd thought about it at all, I'd have imagined him being a carpenter or a bricklayer – going into some sort of trade.

The amazing thing is that this rebel teenager, who had been through all the trauma that's described in the book, was able to turn things round. He was still young, in his early twenties, when he said to me, 'Mum, things are wrong as they are now, and I want to do something. I want to make things better.' He never lost sight of that, and he had the foresight to think and plan to make it happen. He just carried on working towards it until he had created what he's created today.

Yet there were times when I thought that Mark would end up in prison. Even so, I didn't know the half of it: when he was in the worst despair and doing things that he would be ashamed of now, he loved me enough to protect me from all that. I got a few surprises when I read the book.

Even as a little boy he would try to protect me, but I often feel I didn't do enough to protect him. I suppose I'd like to apologise to him for not providing a safe environment for him to grow up in, for all the moving around... But I always loved him, and he always knew that, and he's always loved me.

Now I'm a grandmother, it's a delight to be in his home and to see how relaxed he and his wife Victoria are with their children, and the safe environment they have created for them. It's lovely to be part of that. He's given me so much in my later life.

I think what he's done is incredible. When he first told me his ambition, I must say I thought, 'No, it's impossible for you to get there,' but he's done it. What more can I say? I love him, and I couldn't be more proud of him.

Marion (Mark's mother)

References

Printed sources

Bomber, L., *Inside I'm Hurting: Practical Strategies for Supporting Children with Attachment Difficulties in Schools* (Worth Publishing, 2007).

Bomber, L., and Hughes, D., *Settling Troubled Pupils to Learn: Why Relationships Matter in School* (Worth Publishing, 2013).

Felitti, V.J., Anda, R.F., Nordenberg, D., Williamson, D.F., Spitz, A.M., Edwards, V., Koss, M.P., and Marks, J.S., 'Relationship of Childhood Abuse and Household Dysfunction to Many of the Leading Causes of Death in Adults', *American Journal of Preventive Medicine*, 14/4 (1998), 245–58.

Hauser, S., Allen, J., and Golden, E., *Out of the Woods* (New York: Harvard University Press, 2008).

Hughes, D., and Baylin, J., *Brain-based Parenting: The Neuroscience of Caregiving for Healthy Attachment* (New York: WW Norton, 2012).

Kuypers, L., *The Zones of Regulation: A Concept to Foster Self-regulation and Emotional Control* (San José: Think Social, 2011).

Panksepp, J., *Affective Neuroscience: The Foundations of Human and Animal Emotions* (New York: Oxford University Press, 1998).

Sunderland, M., and Armstrong, N., *The Emotion Cards* (London: Routledge, 2018).

Witcraft, F.E., 'Within my Power', *Scouting Magazine* (1950), 2.

Online sources

Barr, A., 'An Investigation into the Extent to which Psychological Wounds Inspire Counsellors and Psychotherapists to Become Wounded Healers, the Significance of these Wounds on their Career Choice, the Causes of these Wounds and the Overall Significance of Demographic Factors' (The Green Rooms, 2006), http://www.thegreenrooms.net/wounded-healer/

Baylin, J. (2015), *Parental Compassion and Attachment Focused Treatment: Why it's Crucial to Help Parents Resolve their Ambivalence Towards the Mistrusting Child* (DDP Network, 2015), https://ddpnetwork.org/backend

/wp-content/uploads/2015/08/Jon-Baylin-Parental
-Compassion-and-Attachment-Focused-Treatment.-30
-July-2015.pdf

Burke Harris, N., 'How Childhood Trauma Affects
Health Across a Lifetime' [video] (TED talk, 2014),
www.ted.com/talks/nadine_burke_harris_how
_childhood_trauma_affects_health_across_a_lifetime
?language=en

Burt, M., 'What Will it Take to End Homelessness?'
(Washington DC: Urban Institute, 2001), http://
webarchive.urban.org/publications/310305.html

Center on the Developing Child at Harvard University,
'Toxic Stress Derails Health Development' [video]
(2011), https://developingchild.harvard.edu/resources
/toxic-stress-derails-healthy-development

Hughes, D., 'Dyadic Developmental Psychotherapy:
Attachment-focused Treatment for Childhood Trauma'
(2004), http://www.danielhughes.org/p.a.c.e..html

Ludy-Dobson, C.R., and Perry, B.D., 'The Role of
Healthy Relational Interactions in Buffering the Impact
of Childhood Trauma', in E. Gil, ed., *Working with
Children to Heal Interpersonal Trauma: The Power of Play*
(New York: Guilford Press, 2010), https://childtrauma
.org/wp-content/uploads/2014/12/The_Role_of
_Healthy_Relational_Interactions_Perry.pdf.

McLaughlin, K.A., Sheridan, M.A., and Lambert, H.K., 'Childhood Adversity and Neural Development: Deprivation and Threat as Distinct Dimensions of Early Experience', *Neuroscience Biobehavioral Reviews*, 47 (2014), 578–91, https://www.ncbi.nlm.nih.gov/pubmed/25454359

National Scientific Council on the Developing Child, *Excessive Stress Disrupts the Architecture of the Developing Brain: Working Paper 3*, Updated Edition, (Center on the Developing Child, Harvard University, 2005/2014), https://developingchild.harvard.edu/science/key-concepts/executive-function

Neff, K. 'Definition of Self-compassion' (n.d.), https://self-compassion.org/the-three-elements-of-self-compassion-2

Perry, B.D., 'Applying Principles of Neurodevelopment to Clinical Work with Maltreated and Traumatized Children: The Neurosequential Model of Therapeutics', in N. Boyd Webb, ed., *Working with Traumatised Youth in Child Welfare* (New York: Guilford Press, 2006), 27–52, https://childtrauma.org/wp-content/uploads/2013/08/Perry-Bruce-neurosequentialmodel_06.pdf

van der Kolk, B.A., *Developmental Trauma Disorder: Towards a Rational Diagnosis for Children with Complex Trauma Histories* (2005), www.traumacenter.org/products/pdf_files/preprint_dev_trauma_disorder.pdf

DVD

Sunderland, M., *Best Relationship with Your Child* (The Centre for Child Mental Health, in association with Red Shark TV, 2015) [DVD].

Acknowledgements

First, I would like to acknowledge the most important team of people around me: my amazing wife, Victoria Escott, for always loving me and being there for me, and for understanding when my past still affects me in the present; my beautiful stepdaughters Jade, Amber and Jodi for letting me into your lives and teaching me how to love, trust and care; and my gorgeous children Leo and Ava for the joy and healing you give me every day.

I'd like to thank my loving mum and my sister for always being beside me on my journey.

Thanks, too, to all my mentors, guides, coaches and healers. These are the people who have supported me along the way, picked me up when I fell, helped me to overcome my past, taught me that I do matter, believed in my mission, and – most importantly – loved me. You have all contributed in your own ways to my life and my work, and I thank you from the bottom of my heart: Fred Ehresmann, Jon Green, Joanna Hollingbery,

Dick Pennell, Annie Ehresmann, Bell Ehresmann, Stephanie Chivers, Jan Lang, Jeff Bass, Jerry Bowskill, Stella Jeffrey, Colin Sutton, Lynne Pike, Danny Pike, Laura Mulvihill, Julie Hewson, Carol Haywood, Kate Scarlett, Monica Ehresmann, Shoba Manro, Phil Gasson, Tammy Gasson, Ellie Hale, Ian Hale, Mo Cohen, Lucy Pearce, Graham Fisher, Terry Timlett, James Arnold Baker, Jill Bainton, Dave Strudwick, Judith Johnson, Rob Gasson, Daniel Priestley, Verity Ridgman, and all the amazing staff at Life Chance Education and School for Inspiring Talents for all their hard work and commitment supporting our students and families.

Many other people have helped and supported me over the years – too many to mention. You know who you are, and I thank you for your love and support.

The Author

Mark Escott is the co-founder and chief executive officer of Life Chance Education, a therapeutic education provider that specialises in working with young people and families who have experienced trauma (adverse childhood experiences, or ACEs) in their lives. He is committed to transforming the life chances of the people his organisation works with through a growing chain of independent therapeutic day schools – the School for Inspiring Talents – and through his outreach work with the wider community through the ACE Clinic.

A self-described 'poacher turned gamekeeper', Mark had a troubled childhood that led him to drugs and crime, and eventually a spell in a probation hostel. There he was able to witness at first-hand the gulf between those working in the criminal justice and social care systems, and those they were seeking to help.

This marked the start of his commitment to breaking down the language barrier between service providers and service users.

His unique journey has taken him from volunteering with a charity for young people with special needs to becoming an advisory teacher in a behaviour support team. While in this role, he realised that some children were slipping through the net in a conventional school setting and decided to open a school that would meet their needs.

In the School for Inspiring Talents, students find for the first time the unconditional commitment that will convince them that they matter and reveal their potential. Beyond the schools, the multi-disciplinary team that staffs the ACE Clinic offers assessments to young people with a range of emotional and behavioural difficulties and their families, as well as consultation, supervision, training and coaching to professionals in a variety of settings.

Mark hopes to generate a more widespread understanding of ACEs and of the help available to those who have suffered trauma.

Contact

✉ mark.escott@LCEducation.org.uk
🌐 www.LCEducation.org.uk